Soviet Policy
in the
Arc of Crisis

Fred Halliday

IPS

Soviet Policy in the Arc of Crisis

Fred Halliday

© 1981 Fred Halliday and the Institute for Policy Studies.

Published by the Institute for Policy Studies.

Copies of this book are available from the Institute for Policy Studies, 1901
Q Street, N.W., Washington, D.C. 20009 or the Transnational Institute,
Paulus Potterstraat 20, 1071 DA Amsterdam, The Netherlands.

First Printing: 1981

ISBN 0-89758-028-1

ABOUT THE AUTHOR

Fred Halliday was born in Dublin in 1946 and studied at Queen's College, Oxford, and the School of Oriental and African Studies, London. He edited Isaac Deutscher's *Russia, China and the West* (Penguin, 1970) and is author of *Arabia Without Sultans* (Vintage Books, 1975) and *Iran: Dictatorship and Development* (Penguin, 1979), and, with Maxine Molyneux, co-author of *The Ethiopian Revolution* (Verso, 1981).

Fred Halliday speaks Arabic and Persian and has travelled widely in the Arc of Crisis. Since joining the Transnational Institute in 1976, he has visited Iran, Iraq, India, Afghanistan, South Yemen and Ethiopia. His articles have been published in *The New York Times, Los Angeles Times, Newsday, The Nation, In These Times, The Times* (London) and *New Statesman.* An editorial associate of *New Left Review* and *MERIP Reports,* he is currently researching a book on security in the Arabian Peninsula.

TABLE OF CONTENTS

PREFACE

The following study is concerned with an area of the world that is widely regarded as being the center of contemporary international conflict—that range of countries known as the "Arc of Crisis" running from Afghanistan through Iran and the Arab Middle East down to the Horn of Africa. There are many definitions of exactly which area constitutes the "Arc"—like the Bermuda Triangle, it has elastic geographic boundaries, and denotes an anxiety in the human mind as much as a delimited territory. Yet, whatever boundaries are established, it is evident that this range of countries has been the site of immense and as yet unending political upheaval since the mid-1970s.

For many observers and politicians in the West, the underlying cause of turmoil has been the policy of the Soviet Union. It is the connection between regional political developments and Soviet policy in the area which forms the central theme of this text. The Arc of Crisis includes Iran and Afghanistan, Ethiopia and South Yemen, all countries in which changes unwelcome to the United States have taken place in recent years. It includes the Persian Gulf, source of much of the West's oil, and the eastern part of the Arab world, where the Arab-Israeli dispute continues to fester, with grave implications for regional and world peace. Is the central problem in this area that of Soviet policy? Are the Russians "behind" events in the Arc? Does the Soviet rule legitimate the West's new, more forward, stance in the region? These are some of the main questions addressed in the following study.

In focusing upon the nature of Soviet policy, and in advancing a critique of it, I dissent from the view so widely held in the United States and Western Europe that the changes in this area can be understood primarily in terms of an underlying Soviet advance. The thesis of a "Soviet threat" has immense attraction as an explanatory mechanism; my own account cannot claim to have such an appeal. It may, however, bear some closer relationship to what has, in fact, occurred.

The events of the recent years in the Arc of Crisis cannot, by any stretch of the imagination, be regarded as

1

mere past occurrences. There are two particularly forceful reasons for this. First, much of the policy of the present Republican Administration is molded by what its decisionmakers assume to be the lessons of the late 1970s and specifically by what are presented as being the consequences of Soviet "expansion" in Southwest Asia. Secondly, the upheavals in this region are by no means over; the gales of revolution and counter-revolution have not spent themselves. Afghanistan remains in the grip of war. The monarchies of the Arabian Peninsula remain fragile. There is no peace in the Horn of Africa. Most important of all, Iran remains in turmoil, with many pressures upon it from without and within: it is possible that it will go through a period of civil war at some point in the 1980s, and probable that it will become a focus of international tension again. Given this continuing importance of the Arc countries, examination of what has happened there is of continuing relevance.

This study rests upon two assumptions, both of which diverge from the manner in which the issue of Soviet policy in the Arc is conventionally viewed, in the East as well as in the West. The first is an empirical premise: that the sources of political change within these countries lie as much in factors operating within them as they do in the operations of external states, and frequently more so. The disproportionate focus by American commentators upon the role of Soviet policy, like that by Soviet commentators upon the activities of the United States, leads to tendentious analysis. Not only does this perspective misrepresent what has taken place in, say, Iran or Ethiopia; it also leads to a simplistic policy response on the part of the country which feels its strategic influence is threatened—a mistaken belief that a mere re-assertion of geopolitical will can redress the balance.

A second premise is of a prescriptive, policy-oriented, character. The dominant prescriptive approach of almost all Western writing on the subject of the Arc is concerned with its implications for European and American interests and about what "we," i.e. the NATO countries, should do in response to the present crisis. It is this perspective which informs the manner in which a critique of Soviet policy is developed. My policy premise is of a different kind. It seeks to combine analysis of the ways events in the region affect East-West relations with evaluation of the ways major outside powers' policies affect developments within the countries of the region. The two are obviously related at many levels—such matters as an international economic collapse following an interruption of oil supplies, let alone a Third World War, are not issues of indifference to the inhabitants of the Arc. But a definite shift of perspective is nonetheless involved. I would advocate a situation in the Middle East where local states enjoy the maximum realistic conditions for independence, internal democracy and economic development and where they accept each other's legitimate interests. Yet in positing this goal, and in placing both Soviet and U.S. policy in a different perspective, I hope that some alternative policy orientations for Western states may emerge. These are explored in the final section of this work.

The research for this study was carried out under the auspices of the Transnational Institute (TNI) of the Institute for Policy Studies, of which I have been a Fellow since 1975. It is a response to the many stimulating discussions I've attended at the Institute centers in Washington and Amsterdam and to the critical scrutiny to which my analysis has been subjected in these encounters. Sections of this study have already been published as an Institute paper, and in the journal *Race and Class,* and it draws upon other studies of the politics of the region which I have published elsewhere.[1]

As part of this TNI research I have been able to travel to a number of countries in the Arc and to assess, from their individual vantage points, the impact of Soviet policies. These visits include: South Yemen (1977), Ethiopia (1977, 1978), Iran (1979), Iraq (1980), and Afghanistan (1980). Additional research has also been conducted in Western Europe and India, and on several visits to Washington over the same period when it was possible to interview State Department officials and other observers of this region.

I owe a particular word of thanks to the members of the Institute's Militarism and Disarmament Project without whose sustained encouragement this pamphlet would not have been completed. Special gratitude is due to Michael

Klare and Delia Miller for editing the manuscript and preparing it for publication. My thanks are also due to all who read the manuscript in draft stage: to Bob Borosage, Steve Daggett, Saul Landau, and Marcus Raskin, of the Institute; to Makoto Itoh and Maxine Molyneux; and to my colleagues on *New Left Review*, Perry Anderson, Anthony Barnett, and Jon Halliday whose comments were, as always, both astute and substantive.

Fred Halliday
London, May 1981

PART I:
THE RUSSIANS AND
THE MIDDLE EAST

Southwest Asia
(Source: *DOD Annual Report, FY 1982*)

I:
THE ARC: FOCUS OF THE NEW COLD WAR

"Let's not delude ourselves. The Soviet Union underlies all the unrest that is going on. If they weren't engaged in this game of dominoes, there wouldn't be any hot spots in the world."[1]

—Ronald Reagan

The late 1970s witnessed a serious deterioration in the international climate, and particularly in the relations between the United States and the Soviet Union. Yet, while this deterioration began under the Carter Administration, it found an especially clear reflection in the policies of the Reagan Administration which came into office in January, 1981. Such has been the decline in U.S.-Soviet relations that it is legitimate to refer to this period as a New Cold War. While no one can predict the duration of this New Cold War, let alone whether it will or will not lead to a hot war, few can deny the seriousness of the crisis into which relations between the two major world powers have entered.

The Worsening International Climate

The term "Cold War" can be justified by reference to four basic elements in American, and more generally Western, policy during this period. First, many exponents of U.S. foreign policy in the early and mid-1970s had stressed the need and the possibility of moving away from the all-commanding focus on East-West relations. Carter's May, 1977 speech at Notre Dame was a classic statement of this view. Yet, this axis is once again viewed as the center of U.S. foreign policy and the prime international concern of the new Administration. Secondly, there is in both official statements and in other academic and journalistic circles a new emphasis upon a "Soviet threat" and upon the inherently aggressive and "expansionist" nature of the U.S.S.R. Much greater emphasis is now placed upon such issues as Soviet support for "terrorism" than had been evident in earlier years. Thirdly, there is, in the United States in particular, a new stress upon the importance of military power—on the need for increases in military spending, and on the need to be prepared to use military means in response to challenges occurring elsewhere in the world. Fourthly, there is a new emphasis upon the need for greater political and moral unity within Western society as a whole—whether in the realm of family and social values, or within the confines of the Western Alliance. The claim that there exists a mortal threat from without is linked to the call for a new rallying within.

This belief that a New Cold War has begun is by no means confined to the Left. Writing in early 1980, in the aftermath of the Soviet intervention in Afghanistan, former U.S. Ambassador to Moscow George Kennan stated: "Never since World War II has there been so far-reaching a militarization of thought and discourse in the capital."[2] But if this militant mood had taken hold during Carter's Presidency, the four elements of the New Cold War were to find even more forceful expression in the policies and speeches of the new Republican administration that came to office in 1981. Taken together, they betoken a new phase in international relations comparable to the earlier Cold War of the late 1940s and early 1950s. The present Cold War can be termed such because the crisis in international relations is as serious as that earlier one. Such terms as "detente," "disarmament" and even "arms control" sounded singularly out of place in the Washington of early 1981, where the emphasis was upon the need to confront, contain and even "punish" the Russians.

If one examines the themes of the New Cold War as compared to those of the earlier one, however, then an important difference does emerge. In the earlier cases as well as the present there is strong emphasis upon the military danger posed by the Soviet military threat, and it is now argued that the U.S.S.R. has to a considerable extent improved its military position vis-a-vis America (even if the precise nature of this improvement—whether parity or superiority—is in dispute). But this restatement of an earlier theme is accompanied by a significant geopolitical shift, one that highlights the originality of this New Cold War. For the focus of the First Cold War was distinctly Europe, and, in the second instance, the Far East; while the focus of the Second Cold War is Southwest Asia, and in particular the Persian Gulf. It is here that the West is now said to have its major strategic interests, and it is here that the full blast of the Soviet threat is stated to be most evident. For some commentators, the Persian Gulf is now *the* focus of U.S. strategic interests in the world. A Council of Foreign Relations study published in April 1981 stated that the Gulf "presents the single most complex policy task for the United States in meeting Soviet expansionist pressure." An article by Professor Robert Tucker of Johns Hopkins University strikes a similar note: "Almost as certainly as did Europe in the 1940s, the Gulf provides *the* critical source of conflict between the United States and the Soviet Union."[3] This combination of real interests, particularly in oil, and alleged Soviet "misconduct" in the region has produced this focus. Hence events in the Southwest Asian region as a whole have been interpreted both as causing the new deterioration in international relations and as requiring a new Western response, most particularly one in military terms.

Assessment of the New Cold War must therefore involve examination of two major themes: first, the nature of the overall military balance between East and West, and the manner in which perceptions of this in the West changed during the late 1970s; and second, the analysis of changes in Southwest Asia during the same period, and the way in which the West has responded to these changes. The first task lies beyond the scope of this study and has been ably carried out by specialists in the field.[4] Suffice it to say that sober analysis of the facts, and of the manner in which the debate has been conducted, suggests that a significant degree of distortion and exaggeration recurs: misleading comparisons of U.S. and Soviet capabilities are used to produce assessments that are far more alarming than is warranted by the facts. There is a constant usage of ambiguity so that the Soviet Union is made out to be more powerful and more successful than the evidence indicates.

The theme of this study is complementary to those

criticizing alarmist portrayals of the military balance. In both cases, in the military balance and the Arc, it is possible to identify Soviet policy aims and practices and to chart certain Soviet advances. The new climate in the West is not a response to wholly imagined changes or to internal factors alone. But, under closer scrutiny, much of the appears to be tendentious—based upon questionable assumptions, and sometimes on questionable facts; taking individual events out of their local and historical contexts; ignoring the limits on Soviet power and the setbacks encountered by Moscow. In sum, the positing of a "Soviet threat" as an explanatory tool for understanding the events in the Arc during the late 1970s, or as a means of legitimating U.S. policy, cannot survive critical analysis. It is to a considerable extent an illusory picture produced, as is that of an unequal military balance, for reasons of intellectual simplification and, one suspects, considerable political convenience.

It is not, however, sufficient to identify the illusory character of the image of a "Soviet threat" in the Arc. Some alternative explanation for the current crisis in the region, and in international politics generally, has to be offered. If people have mistaken views, they must still hold these views for a reason. There are several historical causes of the New Cold War: some lie in changes in Soviet policy and capability, but others lie in factors within Western society and the Third World itself. Many of the problems for which the New Cold War is supposed to be a response have little to do with the Soviet Union, and nowhere is this more true than in the Arc of Crisis. Analysis of why this region has acquired such special international importance may therefore contribute not only to disentangling the complex changes taking place there, but also to identifying what the broader causes of the New Cold War have been. Soviet policy is one, but only one, of these causes.

The "Threat" to the Persian Gulf

The new emphasis upon the Arc, and the Persian Gulf in particular, is a reflection of at least six trends in international politics during the latter half of the 1970s. Their distinct characters are too often fused into one all-encompassing Soviet "threat." None is specific to the Gulf but each has particular implications for that region. As a means of placing Soviet policy in some context, therefore, we will examine each of these trends briefly before turning to a discussion of the uniquely Soviet contribution to developments in the Gulf.

1. A "Winning Streak" of Third World Revolutions: The latter half of the 1970s witnessed a sustained and geographically diverse series of social upheavals in the Third World which, taken together, entailed a lessening of Western control in the developing areas. To be sure, the First Cold War was also concerned with the U.S. response to revolutionary change in the Third World, when the focus was in the Far East. One important ally was completely lost (China); two further areas were partly conceded, after bitter wars involving a large number of Western troops (Korea and French Indochina); guerrilla movements in other states were crushed (Philippines, Malaya). Elsewhere in the world C.I.A.-supported coups disposed of unwelcome governments (Syria 1949, Iran 1953, Guatemala 1954). At the end of the 1950s there was another round of Third World social upheaval which appeared to threaten the West: the crises in Algeria, Cuba and the Congo (now Zaire) were the highpoints, but the threats were in part contained: the Soviet withdrawal of its rockets from Cuba in October 1962 was the symbolic turning-point. From then onwards the United States was able to operate with considerable freedom in the Third World. All guerrilla movements in Latin America were defeated, and the Allende government in Chile was successfully eliminated in 1973. In Africa there were no major reversals for the West from the early 1960s onwards. The radicalization of the Arab world after Israel's victory in June 1967 proved to be a short-lived affair; the main trend was in a conservative direction. The illusion of a "manageable" Third World was created by over a decade of successful containment.

From 1974 onwards, however, a series of revolutionary and national liberation movements came to power in the Third World, shaking that illusion with unexpected vigor. In Africa, the Ethiopian revolution of 1974 was followed by a series of changes in the remaining embattled colonies   ***11*** attendant upon the revolution in Portugal: in Angola, Mozambique, and Guinea-Bissau (1975) and, as a consequence of the independence of Mozambique, in Zimbabwe (1980). The Southwest Asian region was transformed by the revolutions in Afghanistan (1978) and Iran (1979). In Central America there was a triumphant revolution in Nicaragua (1979), a Left-wing coup in Grenada, and continuing unrest in El Salvador and Guatemala. The psychological impact of these changes served to draw attention to a defeat which had temporarily been repressed in the U.S. consciousness but which continued to exert its subliminal force—the loss of Vietnam, Laos and Cambodia (1975). Had the final defeat in Indochina been an isolated event it might have remained repressed, unmourned and without future policy implications; but the combination of upheavals elsewhere combined to produce what seemed to be an ominous "winning streak" of Third World revolutions to which sooner or later the United States would be forced to respond.

The Persian Gulf became a particularly apt place to respond to this wave of revolutions for three interrelated reasons. *First,* it was geographically near to some of the most important social upheavals of the period—Ethiopia, Iran and Afghanistan. Ethiopia was the site of a large-scale and successful Cuban intervention, in support of the Ethiopian government. Iran was the site of the most humiliating individual incident in the whole process of Third World revolutions—the hostages affair. Afghanistan was the site of a large-scale Soviet military intervention. There was, therefore, more than enough reason for this area to be considered particularly sensitive. But the lessons produced by these events combined with a *second* important factor, namely the fragility of the West's remaining allies in that area, and particularly the vital state of Saudi Arabia. All of the West's allies around the Gulf were monarchies, ruling without the consent of their people and with enormous corruption and inequality of wealth. The events of Iran showed, moreover, that apparently secure regimes could be rapidly overthrown once a popular movement started to grow. Hence the example of Iran created a particular stress upon Western strategy in the region where the structures of monarchical rule were rightly felt to be more frail than had previously been imagined. This frailty

12

would, of course, have been less important had it not been for the *third* reason, the special importance of the Gulf in U.S. global strategy. This is a factor to which we may now turn.

2. The new strategic significance of the Persian Gulf: The Gulf has for decades been a major concern of Western governments. The British government acquired vital interests in Iranian oil before World War I, and the U.S. government declared Saudi Arabia to be a vital U.S. interest during World War II. Yet concern about Persian Gulf oil has risen greatly during the 1970s as a result of two developments. One is that the United States has become a significant importer of oil for the first time. The extent of this dependence should not be exaggerated: only 15 percent of U.S. oil comes from the Gulf, as compared to 60 percent of Europe's and 90 percent of Japan's. But the realization that, for the first time in its history, the United States has become significantly dependent on oil imports has been a cause of growing anxiety. The prosperity of the U.S. economy is, moreover, affected by the greater dependence of the other OECD economies upon Gulf oil: a dramatic slump in their levels of production would inevitably affect U.S. output levels as well. The American oil companies who for decades have controlled the sale of Persian Gulf crude to Europe and Japan would also be direly affected.

The second change has been the growth of a more generalized sense in the advanced industrialized countries that they are dependent on the Third World for vital mineral resources: while there is considerable debate on how true this dependence really is, and how far it is a misinformed alarmism, no one can deny the importance of this new mood of raw material vulnerability. The result of both trends has been a psychological response far in excess of whatever real material reliance has arisen, and a consequent emphasis upon the strategic vulnerability of the United States. The Gulf fits this picture ideally: it produces the most vital of all these raw materials, oil, and it is a long way away. The oil routes run across thousands of miles: the emphasis has consequently been upon the dangers of an interruption in this supply. The emotive language of such strategic concern—with its vocabulary of **13** "life-lines" and "arteries," "choke-points" with "jugulars" —evokes this alarmist perspective.

3. The challenge of OPEC, combined with the economic recession: The rise of the OPEC countries as a major force in international economic affairs dates from late 1973, when, after the outbreak of the fourth Arab-Israeli war, the Arab QPEC states increased their prices and imposed a temporary oil embargo. Significant price increases have followed, and have been seen in the West as a major cause of the recession of the latter half of the 1970s. The outstanding feature of this recession in comparison to previous ones has been that it combined a falling off in industrial output with inflation. The latter phenomenon, which affects all sectors of society, has been widely blamed upon the actions of OPEC. This attribution of blame is far too simple, but, as with the "Soviet threat," it has an immediate appeal. It reinforces a feeling at the popular level that "something should be done" about the Arab oil producers, which is matched at the level of strategic planning by a consciousness of the new vulnerability which OPEC has brought about. Combined with resentment within the United States at the treatment of the hostages held in Iran until January 1981, it has been a significant factor in fostering a Cold War mood at the popular level. The cause of U.S. weakness at home— inflation produced by greedy oil states—is easily associated with a major source of humiliation abroad—the Iranian revolution and the activities of the OPEC bloc.

4. The erosion of U.S. control over its major capitalist allies: While the United States remains by far the most powerful economic entity within the Western Alliance, its dominance has been gradually eroded. In 1950, U.S. GNP accounted for about 50 percent of total world GNP; in 1980 the figure had sunk to 30 percent and by 2000 is expected to be 20 percent. In 1978, GNP per capita in the United States, at $9,770, was below that of Switzerland, Denmark, Sweden and West Germany.[5] This output change has been accompanied by other more visible signs of U.S. slippage: the emergence of a U.S. balance of payments deficit at the height of the Vietnam War; the decline of the dollar in relation to other currencies; and, in the late 1970s, the inroads into U.S. domestic markets of Japanese imports. In military terms, the United States has, if anything, lengthened its lead over its major capitalist allies. But it is this combination of a sustained imbalance in military power along with a closing of the civilian economic gap that has underlain the growing policy disunity in the Western Alliance. In the 1960s it was only Gaullist France which defied the United States: by the late 1970s Western Europe as a whole was reluctant to follow U.S. policies, as demonstrated in European failure to back U.S. moves over Afghanistan and Iran. Outside Europe, both Japan and Canada harbored growing resistance to U.S. policies, which combined with reassertive nationalism in those two countries.

While a considerable amount of the U.S. response to this problem was directed at relations between Washington and the allies—within NATO and in negotiations over trade with Japan—some was directed at the Gulf. For, in Washington's view, a reassertion of the U.S. military presence in the Gulf would remind the Europeans and Japanese of just *who* it was who protected their interests in this critical area. At the same time, it served to head off whatever independent initiatives these states might be seeking to undertake in the region on the Arab-Israeli dispute. After all, the Middle East, and the Gulf in particular, has long been the site of conflict between the Europeans and the United States, both at the state-to-state level and in competition between the oil companies. In recent years there has been considerable friction in transatlantic relations as a result of initiatives taken by either Europe or the United States which the other sees as undermining its influence: on occasion, Arab states have sought to take advantage of this, as in Saudi threats to buy French or German arms as opposed to U.S. equipment. The disagreements over Afghan and Iranian policies, coupled with the European initiative on Palestine in June 1980, brought this awareness to the surface. Focusing on the Gulf is therefore valuable in a number of respects: it hints at a U.S. control over the vital oil supplies; it indicates that Europe may no longer be the center of U.S. strategic concern; and it warns against unruly European initiatives. **15**

When this is combined with the need for NATO to develop an extra-European capacity, the projection of U.S. military force into the Gulf becomes one important means of re-establishing a general discipline within the Western Alliance.

5. *The quest for higher appropriations by the U.S. military:* The U.S. military machine was pressing for increased appropriations throughout the latter part of the 1970s, and, with the advent of the Reagan Administration, appears to have won its campaign decisively. U.S. military expenditure is now scheduled to rise from $162 billion in 1981 to $343 billion in 1986. A major component of the military expansion is in Third World intervention forces—these account for some 25 percent of U.S. military expenditure, far more than the amount devoted to nuclear weapons. The defeat in Indochina has obviously been one factor which, through a delayed psychological boomerang, has influenced thinking on this matter. So has increased Soviet military activity in the Third World—whether by assisting Cuban forces in Angola and Ethiopia, or by sending its own forces into Afghanistan. The emphasis upon Third World intervention and on desert combat became a major fashion in U.S. military circles by 1980. The Gulf is an ideal target for such interventions: the threat of an interruption to oil is taken seriously; the very refusal of local states to allow U.S. forces to be stationed there means that a far greater emphasis has to go into the technology of "rapid deployment"; the fact that such forces may be used not against the Russians but against Arabs and Persians is not, in the light of earlier considerations on OPEC and the hostages, a restraining factor. For strategic planners the Gulf region has another important military attraction: it adjoins the Soviet Union. Emphasis in the Carter and Reagan Administrations upon the need to "project" U.S. force along this southern flank of the U.S.S.R. has been, in some sections of the Administrations, as important as the specific need to protect oil.[6]

6. *The increased power and strategic projection of the Soviet Union:* Throughout the 1970s the Soviets have lost influence in the Middle East and have seen three of their closest allies turn to the West: Egypt, Iraq and Somalia. But they have also gained influence in Ethiopia and Afghanistan, and have benefitted, by default, from the U.S. defeat in Iran. The increased visibility of the U.S.S.R. has reflected a broader shift in international relations: the Soviet Union has attained rough parity in the military balance with the United States, and thus has increasingly felt itself entitled to act as a major power in world affairs. Indeed there is a striking symmetry between the parity which the U.S.S.R. is now acquiring in military power and that in Third World influence: there is also a symmetry in the U.S. response, which is to see the attainment of parity by the Russians as itself a challege to detente. For the previous conception of detente presupposed a U.S. superiority in both these domains: the trends of the latter half of the 1970s have weakened that superiority in Third World terms, and have largely ended it in strategic nuclear terms. While this change in Soviet capacity is, as already indicated, by no means the only reason for the New Cold War and the particular emphasis on the Gulf, it is nonetheless an important factor. It will be examined in greater detail in Chapter II.

The "threat" posed to the Gulf cannot, therefore, be reduced to any single trend. It is rather a composite response reflecting a variety of causes and purposes. As is often the case in debates on strategy, the psychological component, based on anxiety and a foreshortened sense of geography, can weigh far more than an informed study might justify. Such strategic alarmism is common enough in discussions on the Third World. British and French obsession about the Suez Canal led to the disastrous attack on Egypt in 1956. The U.S. Congressional debate on the Panama Canal Treaty in 1978 betrayed a similar sense of vulnerability. Instead of acknowledging these psychological factors, public debate has tended to concentrate upon the simplest explanatory factor, the Soviet threat. By compressing geography, Soviet advances in Afghanistan or Ethiopia are seen as threatening the Gulf itself: such interpretations ignore the fact that the easiest way for Russia to hit at Western assets and communications lines in the Gulf is by rocket and air strikes from bases within **17**

Soviet territory. The threat posed by OPEC to the Western economies is further associated with the advantages gained by the U.S.S.R. The unrequited humiliations of Vietnam and the hostages affair find expression in a new preparedness for military intervention in the Third World. The very real loss of control in parts of the Third World, coupled with the sense of a need to reassert American power, has generated this new Gulf policy. It is out of these overlapping concerns that the "Soviet threat" to the Gulf has been produced.

The antecedents of current anxiety on the Gulf go back a long way. In the 1790s, Britain sent warships to dissuade the Sultan of Muscat from granting facilities to Napoleon who, from his expeditionary base in Egypt, was seen as threatening the sea route to India. In the latter part of the nineteenth century, the Middle East was the focus of intense rivalries between Britain and Germany, and between both the Russian Czars: indeed Russophobia in that period centered on what was then called "The Eastern Question." After World War I, British policy in the Middle East was shaped by what was thought to be a Bolshevik threat coming over the Caucasus and the Hindu Kush; and it was in Iran, in 1946, that the first major confrontation of the First Cold War—concerning the presence of Soviet troops—occurred. From the mid-1950s onward, Western anxiety centered on Soviet influence in Egypt and, more generally, on the Soviet role in the Arab-Israeli dispute.

Strategic concern about the Gulf began to grow in the early 1970s, as the British withdrew their main forces from the Gulf in 1971 and the OPEC states exerted their newfound power in 1973. In response to these developments there emerged some of the first Western counter-measures: the initial suggestions of a need for Western military intervention in the Gulf voiced in 1974, and the establishment of a common front of Western consumers in the face of OPEC which led to the establishment of the International Energy Agency in 1976.[7] Although little attention was paid to it at the time, a decision was also taken in the early 1970s to build up the naval facilities on the British-owned Indian Ocean island of Diego Garcia. And, consistent with the "Nixon Doctrine," great emphasis was laid on the need to build up regional forces capable of undertaking a security role; in the Gulf proper, Washington's choice naturally fell upon the apparently secure ruler of Iran, Mohammad Reza Pahlavi.

As the 1970s proceeded, it is possible to detect a steadily growing strategic concentration on the Gulf: U.S. anxiety about the old focus of Soviet influence, Egypt, declined as Cairo's relations with Moscow worsened, while the winding down of the Indochina wars led to a gradual shift in Asian strategic perspective westwards that was already noticeable in 1973.[8] By the mid-1970s, Iran and Saudi Arabia had become the principal customers for U.S. arms, and then Secretary of State Henry Kissinger was meeting regularly with the Shah to coordinate joint security measures in the Gulf area.

The turning-point came in 1978, when U.S. policymakers were faced with a range of new challenges: the Soviet and Cuban effort to assist Ethiopia in repulsing the Somali invasion became public knowledge in January 1978, and provoked grave anxiety in Washington; then followed the communist coup in Afghanistan in April; and by September the revolutionary movement in Iran had gathered full force. Before the end of the year Carter's National Security Adviser Brzezinski had coined the phrase "Arc of Crisis" to denote the range of countries in South and Southwest Asia where the threat was posed. "An Arc of crisis stretches along the shores of the Indian Ocean, with fragile social and political structures in a region of vital importance to us threatened with fragmentation. The resulting political chaos could well be filled by elements hostile to our values and sympathetic to our adversaries."[9] Brzezinski was further quoted as saying: "I'd have to be blind or Pollyanish not to recognize that there are dark clouds on the horizon."[10] The press joined in this debate with its own strategic geometry: the *Economist* talked of "the crumbling triangle" bounded by Kabul in Afghanistan, Ankara in Turkey, and Addis Ababa in Ethiopia. *Time* magazine preferred "The Crescent of Crisis" which, bulging north-westwards to include Egypt, Israel and Syria, was portrayed on its front cover being devoured by the Russian bear.[11]

During the course of 1978 the focus of world tension shifted uneasily between the Southwest Asian and African contexts: the latter was already prominent in alarmist views because of the crisis in Angola in 1975-1976 and the two invasions of the Shaba province of Zaire from rebel bases in Angola in 1977-1978. In both cases Cuban forces were said to be involved. Cuba certainly had sent forces to Angola, but, as Congressional hearings were to show, the dispatch of Cuban forces in November 1975 was to protect the government of the newly independent state against attacks in which both the C.I.A. and South Africa had already become deeply implicated. Cuban involvement in the Shaba affair, although greatly emphasized in the U.S. press at the time, turned out to be unsubstantiated. Nevertheless, presented through the prism of a decomposing Third World, Angola and Shaba appeared to confirm the view that a revolutionary wave, impelled by Moscow, was sweeping through Asia and Africa.[12]

One of the most cogent statements of this strategic alarm came from former Secretary of State Henry Kissinger. In December 1978, Mr. Kissinger talked of what he called "the geopolitical decline from Vietnam through Angola, Ethiopia, South Yemen and Afghanistan" which had, he said, "demoralized friends and emboldened enemies." In testimony before the House of Representatives on the SALT-II Treaty, Kissinger talked about "an unprecedented Soviet assault on the international equilibrium" and listed what he saw as the instances of this assault. "They are not, to be sure, all controlled by Moscow; but someone who has started a rockslide cannot avoid responsibility by claiming that the rock he threw was not the one that ultimately killed bystanders. These tactics, reinforced by a Soviet military build-up threatening the strategic, theater and conventional balances, are incompatible with any notion of detente or coexistence."[13]

Whatever the situation at the end of 1978, it cannot be said to have improved over the next two years. In January 1979, the Iranian revolution reached its climax: the Shah fled and Khomeini returned in triumph. A month later fighting broke out along the border between North and South Yemen and the Carter Administration rushed $380 million worth of military equipment to North Yemen, the country which was seen as the current front line against communist "expansionism"; the somewhat artificial nature of this crisis only emerged later (see Chapter IV). After a temporary lull, U.S.-Iranian relations reached a new low when the U.S. Embassy in Tehran was seized on November 4, 1979. A few days later, on November 20, Islamic rebels seized the Holy Mosque in Mecca, thereby throwing the stability of Saudi Arabia into question. On December 24, Soviet forces entered Afghanistan in large numbers. In the face of these developments, the incumbent Administration produced what became known as the "Carter Doctrine." In his State of the Union message on January 23, 1980, the President stated: "Any attempt by any outside force to gain control of the Persian Gulf region will be regarded as an assault on the vital interests of the United States of America, and such an assault will be repelled by any means necessary, including military force."

To implement the new doctrine, the Administration brought forward plans for what was then termed the Rapid Deployment Force and sought military bases in the area. Yet many of Carter's critics considered his response as being too weak and too belated: he was blamed for the failures in Iran, Afghanistan and Ethiopia. He lost considerable support because of his inability to do anything about the detention of the U.S. hostages in Iran. These specific criticisms combined with a more general sense that the United States had lost ground in world affairs because of a decline of national "will." Many of these commentators concentrated specifically on the Gulf: Professor Tucker of Johns Hopkins stressed the need for a U.S. military presence in the Gulf area, while Dr. John Kelly called for a Western counter-offensive against OPEC.[14] Others raked over the coals of U.S. defeats to discern alternative courses of action that would have prevented the triumph of America's enemies. Carter and Brzezinski did indeed respond to this mood and in many instances laid the bases of what was to be policy of their successors. But it was not sufficient. In 1981, a new administration came to power, bringing a commitment to shore up U.S. power in the Gulf and to combat what it described as persistent Soviet "expansionism."

Because the Gulf will continue to be a major focus of U.S. foreign policy and a likely pivot of U.S.-Soviet relations, it is essential that we examine the Arc countries closely, and try to determine what has actually occurred there. Chapter II discusses Soviet foreign policy in general, in an attempt to provide a general background to the particular initiatives taken by Moscow in the region. Chapters III and IV consider two components of Soviet policy: the importance of the region to the U.S.S.R. on the one hand, and Soviet relations with the Arab world on the other. In Part II, we will examine the upheavals in the Arc of Crisis itself, and especially in the four countries conventionally signalled as being the sites of major Soviet advances: Ira, Afghanistan, South Yemen, Ethiopia. Chapters V, VI and VII provide an alternative explanation of the turmoil in these states, and of what affect Soviet and U.S. policies have had there. Finally, the conclusion summarizes the main findings of the study with regard to Soviet policy, and suggests the basic elements of a more balanced Western approach.

Before proceeding to these specific discussions, however, it may be appropriate to identify the key assumptions regarding Soviet policy in the Arc which permeate most Western thinking on the topic, and which underlie the Reagan Administration's strategic response. As we shall discover, many of these assumptions are of dubious foundation. (The bracketed references after each one indicate where the argument is developed in the subsequent text.) But because these themes recur with such frequency, it is useful first to examine them here:

Seven Questionable Assumptions

1. Soviet instigation: Many analysts argue that the Soviet Union was in some way responsible for initiating the changes that have been taking place in the Arc. A "hard" version of this text is Reagan's claim that the Soviet Union "underlies all the unrest that is going on." Mr. Kissinger's version is a "soft" one, allowing that the Russians have not "controlled" all the events in the region; but this is only a feint, since he still asserts that the Russians "started" the rockslide of revolutions, and that they have been engaged in an "assault"—a deliberate, continuous act. Closer examination will show, however, that not one of the major upheavals alluded to in the Arc discussion was instigated by the Russians (Chapter V).

2. Soviet benefit: Even if the U.S.S.R. did not initiate these changes, it can be argued that the Russians have benefitted from them, and have, wherever possible, taken advantage of them. Senator Henry Jackson has compared Soviet policy to that of a thief in a hotel, walking along the corridors trying every bedroom door to see if one is open. Much discussion focuses on Soviet "risk-taking" in pursuit of such openings. There is some validity to the argument that the Russians have gained advantage from change in the Arc: Ethiopia and Afghanistan are cases in point. But when the final balance sheet is drawn up, we will discover that the Russians haven't gained all that much ground, since they have in the same period suffered many reverses of which the West has taken advantage. Indeed, both major world powers normally seek to take advantage of changes within specific Third World countries (Chapter IV).

3. Soviet misconduct: From 1978 onwards, U.S. officials have stressed that the U.S.S.R. has "violated" the rules of detente and that such misbehavior will result in a U.S. policy of "linkage," whereby Soviet policy in one area of the world will be judged as helpful or unhelpful for East-West negotiation as a whole. As we shall discover this is a dubious approach. To begin with, the Soviet Union has on some occasions exercised restraint in situations in which it could have pressed its advantage. Moreover, Moscow has sometimes offered to negotiate with Washington on issues of mutual concern. It was often the United States which refused such negotiations; whether for good or bad reasons is not the question here. Finally, those practices which are said to constitute Soviet "misconduct" can, in a historical perspective, be seen as repeating forms of practice which the West has allowed itself for a very long time. As in the military balance, so in Third World policy: the charge of a Soviet "advantage" or "misconduct" appears to rest not upon a breach of mutually accepted rules but rather upon an underlying reluctance to grant the U.S.S.R. parity as a major world power (Chapter VI).[15]

4. Soviet responsibility for ending detente: Many   **23**

Western commentators claim that the Russian intervention in Ethiopia or Iran or Afghanistan destroyed detente; Brzezinski has stated that detente "lies buried in the sands of Ogaden"—the region of Ethiopia where the fighting took place in early 1978;[16] Senator Charles Percy sought, in February 1979, to link SALT-II to what he claimed was Soviet responsibility for the "chaos" in Iran.[17] Yet the briefest retrospective will show that Soviet-U.S. relations began to deteriorate much earlier than is now supposed: the officials now advising the Reagan Administration were calling for a tougher line against the Soviet Union from the mid-1970s onwards. It was then that the Committee on the Present Danger, Team B, and other more hawkish forces began to make their appearance. The SALT-II Treaty was in trouble long before Afghanistan became an issue in East-West relations. Few can doubt that the Soviet intervention there worsened the international climate, but it is relevant to remember how far it had already deteriorated before that time.[18]

5. *The Soviet thirst for oil:* The Soviet "energy crisis" is believed to offer a plausible rationale for recent foreign policy conduct, and in particular for a Soviet interest in the Gulf. This is commonly cited in Western discussions, and has been picked up by some of the more conservative Arab states. Yet there is no reason to conclude that this has an influence upon Soviet policy in the region. As we shall see, the Russians do not need large quantities of Gulf oil; they know, moreover, that any attempt to seize the Gulf could trigger World War III (Chapter III).

6. *"Surrogates" and "proxies" of Soviet policy:* It is stock-in-trade of much analysis that the U.S.S.R. is able to control the policies of its allies in the region and that they act at the behest of Moscow in all major matters. Just as Cuba and Vietnam are seen as "surrogates" in their actions, so Libya, South Yemen and the PLO are seen as Soviet clients in the Middle East. However, it should be evident from the record of Middle East politics that the Soviet Union does not truly control the policies of the countries allied with it: if it did, it would not have been thrown out of Egypt, or forced to send its forces into

24

Afghanistan. The United States has had enough problems with its allies; we will find that Moscow is no better placed to determine what *its* associates in the region do.

7. An alternative U.S. policy: Many critics of the Carter Administration have argued that Washington could have pursued different, more hard-line policies in the Gulf area. All that was needed to protect U.S. interests, they assert, was an exertion of "will." Podhoretz's *The Present Danger* is a good example of this reasoning; yet it is a curiously vacuous analysis, devoid of substantive argument or examination of the events it bewails. There is no recognition of either the real and increasing limits on U.S. power, or of the local conditions in the world outside upon which U.S. effectiveness is dependent. Podhoretz's call for a return to the containment policy of the late 1940s is an ahistorical pipe-dream. Attempts to rewrite history in the Right-wing revisionist vein on Iran and OPEC are similarly idealist.[19] It is noticeable that those who berated Carter on Afghanistan, the hostages, and Ethiopia fought shy of stating explicitly what *they* would actually have done. Both the Americans and the Russians have experienced the limits of power in the Third World. Hard-line second-guessing may be convenient for discrediting incumbent presidents; it is no guide to analyzing recent history, or to laying the basis for future policy (See Conclusion for a more realistic approach).

Enough has been said to indicate that there is much to question in the prevailing assumptions on the Arc of Crisis. Yet real and important changes have been taking place in the region over the past few years, and there have been significant changes in Soviet foreign policy as well. The chapters that follow are devoted to the attempt to provide a credible and comprehensive explanation of these processes.

II:

SOVIET FOREIGN POLICY: AN OVERVIEW

Any discussion of Soviet policy in the Middle East has to consider more general issues of Moscow's role in world affairs, and to relate the two.[1] This forms the subject of the present chapter. Most analysis of Soviet policy in this particular region tends to assume certain global premises and to use the Middle East as an illustration of them. Thus, for many critics in the West, Soviet policy is assumed to be expansionist and aggressive, and cases are adduced from the Arab world or Afghanistan to prove this. Often, Soviet actions are explained by reference to a supposed blueprint for world domination. On the other side, the Soviets present themselves as peace-loving, respectful of the principles of non-interference, and eager to assist progressive forces. For the Chinese, the Soviet Union behaves as a "hegemonic," or imperialist power. In all of these cases, individual incidents of Soviet policy in the region may be used to reinforce a particular view of Soviet conduct, but they are rarely used to correct one.

This deductive approach therefore prejudges the evidence of what the Russians have actually done in these countries, and it leaves open the question of how far Soviet policy is one that can be seen as inimical to the West. Soviet policy is not wholly disinterested, nor is it abstentionist: where opportunities for advancing Soviet interests arise these may be taken. But this does not mean that the Soviet Union acts according to some long-term blueprint, let alone that events in any particular area go according to such a blueprint. There is no Central Threat Office in the Kremlin, no body directing and coordinating an attack on the West resulting in the political upheavals and political conflicts of recent years. Terms such as "targets" of Soviet policy, "assault" upon the international order, or "encirclement" of the Gulf present a misleading and schematic view of what Russian policy is about. Yet there are certain ways in which Soviet policy *is* competitive with that of the West and will remain so, within the limits of whatever global agreements on detente may be achieved. There are also ways in which Soviet policy is changing, as we shall learn later in this chapter. Let us begin, however, with a general discussion of Soviet foreign policy.

The General Aims of Soviet Policy

If one seeks a general view of Soviet policy, a good way to start is by looking at the Soviet Constitution. This is a significant source not because states always do what their constitutions ordain—the Soviet one allows for the free secession of constituent republics and other democratic rights which no one can seriously claim are ever implemented or respected—but because the Soviet Constitution lays down the general guidelines of Soviet foreign policy. It also enables us to identify two key aspects of that policy: the *variety* of goals, and the *hierarchy* of these goals. Thus Article 28 of the 1977 Soviet Constitution reads: "The U.S.S.R. steadfastly pursues a Leninist policy of peace and stands for strengthening of the security of nations and broad international cooperation. The foreign policy of the U.S.S.R. is aimed at ensuring international conditions favorable for building communism in the U.S.S.R., safeguarding the state interests of the Soviet Union, consolidating the positions of world socialism, supporting the struggle of peoples for national liberation and social progress, preventing wars of aggression, achieving universal and complete disarmament, and consistently implementing the principle of the peaceful co-existence of states with different social systems. In the U.S.S.R. war propaganda is banned."[2]

What emerges from this is that there is a clear Soviet commitment to consolidating their own social system and to assisting those elsewhere in the world who are seeking to build similar societies. But this aim is offset by other goals—preserving the security of the U.S.S.R., and seeking a reduction in tension and arms rivalry between itself and the West. The Soviet Union considers itself to be a major power in the world and to be entitled to pursue policies consonant with that importance. It is not, however, going to prejudice world peace or negotiation with the West in a reckless manner. It is within the limits imposed by these two sets of commitments that the Russians pursue their foreign policy, and it is within the same limits that the West can seek to reach a measure of agreement with the U.S.S.R. on matters of vital interest. A degree of competition will, however, necessarily remain, as the goals of the Constitution make clear.

The dimensions of this competition with the West can be spelled out in the following terms:

(1) The Soviet Union sees itself as part of a world system that is in competition with the capitalist world system and which will, sooner or later, prevail over it. This is a general philosophical concern. It is on a par with the American commitment to the survival and extension of the "free world." If President Reagan feels entitled to predict the end of communism, as "a sad bizarre chapter in human history whose last pages are even now being written," President Brezhnev clearly feels himself entitled to similar reflections about the capitalist world.

(2) The Soviet Union is ideologically committed to supporting what it sees as progressive forces in the world. This is not an aim that it can pursue in the face of objective constraints, or would choose to do at the risk of provoking war. Indeed, Soviet governments have more often than is usually remembered *failed* to live up to this goal: Stalin's abandonment of the Greek communists, and Brezhnev's trifling support for the Popular Unity government in Chile, are cases in point. On the other hand, this principle is sometimes used to justify support for regimes that are not revolutionary—that are either straightforwardly reactionary (Idi Amin of Uganda, Jorge Videla of Argentina) or which, while exhibiting some progressive characteristics, are not as far to the left as the Russians for a time maintain (Sukarno's Indonesia, Nasser's Egypt). It is therefore less of an outright revolutionary commitment than the Russians or their right-wing critics claim.

(3) The Soviet Union is concerned to develop state-to-state relations with as wide a range of countries as possible, irrespective of their political structures. In a world where **28** revolution is not a simultaneous process, traditional diplo-

macy remains an important part of international activity, designed to advance the interests of the Soviet Union as a state.

(4) The Soviet Union aims to have a global military capability. It has been building a naval fleet capable of sailing in all the main waters of the world, and it has developed a long-range air capability—as demonstrated by the 1977 airlift to Ethiopia. Its global capability is still smaller than that of the United States, and its network of overseas facilities (with the exception of those in Eastern Europe) is, in comparison with that of America, diminutive.[3] But the aim of strategic parity within all spheres is a constant.

These general considerations apply to the U.S.S.R.'s world posture, as well as to its policy in any particular area. As indicated, they imply that the Soviet foreign policy outlook is not a passive one. But there are other considerations that limit any Soviet initiative. The Russians retain a strong interest in security. Moscow has an ideological reason for this concern—the belief that the capitalist world would like to weaken and, if possible, destroy the Soviet system. This is not just an abstract theoretical tenet: the Bolsheviks were attacked by a dozen foreign countries in 1918-20, and the U.S.S.R. just survived the Second World War—incurring the loss of at least twenty million lives in the process. Since then, the Russians feel that they have been encircled by American bases and treaty organizations. In Europe this Soviet concern for security is guaranteed by the *cordon sanitaire* of Warsaw Pact countries. In the Middle East it has been expressed in Soviet willingness to reach accommodations with any stable government that will do business with it, whether it be socialist in orientation or a conservative monarchy—as in Iran up to 1979 under the Shah, or Afghanistan up to 1973 under King Zahir. Moscow also seeks to develop trading and military links with these countries, again irrespective of their political hue. Its largest trading partner in the Middle East was, until his fall in 1979, the Shah of Iran. These links not only increase Soviet influence, but also enable it to gain some benefit from foreign trade in strictly economic terms.

A second, related, concern is the stability of the region. **29**

The Russians know that instability often affects them negatively. It provides opportunities for anti-communist forces to gain advantage, and for Western states to promote their strategic interests. Instability also exposes them to difficult choices—of whether to intervene or not. Failure to do so involves loss of prestige and a gain for their enemies; intervention has risks in the country concerned, and in the wider context of Soviet-American relations. Provided there is stability the Russians are quite prepared to collaborate with the *least* revolutionary of regimes. But, once that stability goes, they will try to preserve or advance their interests, in the more fluid situation that results.

A third major constraint upon Soviet policy is the limited level of resources which it can deploy in pursuit of its foreign objectives. This level has certainly increased in recent years; such an expansion in military capacity, rather than any change in Soviet strategy, has made possible the military aid given to such states as Angola, Vietnam, and Ethiopia. But the Russians are still constrained in what they can supply, particularly in the economic field. They are short of foreign exchange. They are deficient in modern technology. They can certainly not provide on a regular basis one of the major requirements of countries in the arid Middle East—food. Even what they have provided has been the subject of considerable criticism in the recipient countries because of its poor technical quality. And they face a problem, vague but nonetheless forceful, with their own people. The Soviet populace, on available evidence, resent the level of assistance given to foreign countries and blame this assistance for the consumer shortages at home. In the past such resentment focused on Soviet aid to China and Cuba. Later on it was assistance to Egypt. It was ironic that because of popular resentment the press had to downplay the Soviet role in the highly successful airlift of emergency food aid to avert the Cambodian famine of 1979-80.[4]

Finally, and encompassing all of the above reasons, the Russians want to achieve a permanent working relationship with the West: to avert war, to manage crisis situations, and to derive maximum support for their own economic development programs. The Russians are not going to abandon the political bases of their system: neither the monolithic system of one-party rule internally, nor the general rivalry with capitalism internationally. But they are aware of their own economic limitations, and within these given political limits have shown themselves more than willing to negotiate and fulfill agreements of a comprehensive character, such as SALT and nuclear test ban treaties. While they will certainly take initiatives where no agreements exist, the Russians have not shown interest in prejudicing these general agreements on arms control for regional advantage. They have indeed tried to extend them with further agreements on particular regions such as the Gulf and the Indian Ocean—initiatives that the West has rejected. Moreover, the pattern of their conduct in the Middle East has often showed restraint, both in their own actions and those of their allies—even when, by holding back the Arabs vis-a-vis Israel or the Ethiopians vis-a-vis the Somalis, they have incurred the displeasure of these allies in so doing.

These central concerns of Russian policy mean that the U.S.S.R. *has* interests in the Middle East, and will act to defend them. But the existence of such interests does not substantiate the alarmist case. The argument that there has always been an expansionist drive or a recent radical shift in Soviet policy is without foundation: as already suggested, it was not the Russians who overthrew the Emperor of Ethiopia or the Shah of Iran. The development of conflict situations in these countries was wholly a result of endogenous developments.

Indeed, these developments have usually worried Moscow as much as they have worried Washington. The Russian perception of the Middle East in the postwar era has been a continuously disappointing and alarming one. Their attempts to find permanent allies amongst nationalist regimes there have almost all failed: their more recent allies are either insignificant (South Yemen), or precarious and costly (Afghanistan, Ethiopia). They feel that their junior allies in the Arab world have been unreliable, and have often engaged in adventurist policies which have prejudiced Soviet security. While the rise of such regimes has provided them with some temporary openings, as has the revolution in Iran, they see that relations with such governments can also be risky. This is so, both in terms of

East-West relations as a whole, and in terms of the consequences which such regimes may have for local communist parties.

The alarm which the Russians have felt about the Middle East is, however, most related to the fact that the uncertain politics of the region offers openings for the West to consolidate itself strategically in the area. The events of 1980 provided a good example of this: both the Iranian seizure of U.S. hostages, and the Iran-Iraq war provided the United States with the opportunity to increase its military presence in the area. The U.S. Navy increased its forces in the waters around the Gulf, while the Air Force sent reconnaissance planes to reassure Saudi Arabia. This link between the political turmoil of the region and the strategic projection of the West has taken an added twist in recent years because of technical advances in missile launching. In the late 1940s and 1950s, the Soviet fear focussed on the West's use of air and land bases in the Middle East for actions against the U.S.S.R. in the event of a world war. Now U.S. submarines deployed in the Indian Ocean can launch missiles directly against the U.S.S.R., a development which has opened a totally new flank of vulnerability for Soviet strategic planners.

Soviet Policy in the 1970s: New Dimensions

So far, Soviet policy has been treated in a relatively constant fashion as reflecting stable and persistent concerns of geography and political strategy. There is indeed a great element of stability in such Soviet thinking: the lessons of history are carefully studied in the Kremlin; the very personal continuity of the Brezhnev era, spanning nearly twenty years, confirms this. Yet, within the ambit of these general policy lines, it is possible to discern a number of shifts in the 1970s, which both affect and are affected by developments in the Arc of Crisis.

1. Increased military capacity: Since the early 1960s, the Soviet Union has been steadily closing the gap in the military balance between itself and the West, so that by the late 1970s a condition of rough parity prevailed. This is

an important source of confidence to the Soviet Union—
and a corresponding source of alarm to the West. Such a
process, reflecting decisions taken in the early 1960s, would
inevitably have occurred sooner or later, given the growing
economic and scientific power of the U.S.S.R. But the
pursuit of parity may well have received additional impetus
from what were perceived as major foreign policy defeats in
that period—precisely those turning-points which opened
the era of apparent U.S. domination in the Third World
stretching from 1962 to 1974. Three such defeats are worth
listing: the loss of China, which opened a vast new area of
uncertainty on the Eastern frontiers; the forced withdrawal
of the missiles from Cuba in October 1962; and the inability
to aid the revolutionary forces in the Congo. These setbacks
certainly contributed to the fall of Khrushchev. They must
also have strengthened the determination of Soviet military and political leaders to be able, in the future, to retain
those advantages in the Third World which were under
threat. As a result, the Russians were in a far better position
by the mid-1970s, and thus could take initiatives that they
were technically and politically unable to take in the early
1960s. They had already shown, by their aid to Vietnam,
that they were prepared and able to empower a revolutionary movement in the Third World to confront the
United States in a sustained manner. They also showed, in
the Egypt of the late 1960s, that they were willing to send
thousands of Soviet servicemen to help defend a Third
World country. The aid to Angola and Ethiopia, and the
firm commitment to Afghanistan in the late 1970s, followed.

2. Greater caution on Third World nationalism:
Despite their increased ability to provide military support
to revolutionary regimes in the Third World, the Russians
have been faced with many setbacks as a result of the
internal political development of these states. The classic
case was Egypt where, after years of Soviet support and
investment, the Sadat leadership expelled the Russians in
the mid-1970s. Similar cases have occurred in Somalia and
Iraq, and there have been numerous instances of left
nationalist pro-Soviet regimes being overthrown (Ghana,
Indonesia, Mali, etc.). Either the internal evolution of these
regimes, or their vulnerability to coups, can lead to Soviet   **33**

reversals. As a result there has been an apparent shift in Soviet attitudes to the Third World, away from the advocacy of the "non-capitalist road," the model of radical nationalism and state domination of the economy which was expected to lead towards socialism. As one expert, Professor Jerry Hough, has written: "Some Soviet scholars argue that in most Third World countries there are powerful forces working against continued socialistic development over the medium term . . . officials in the governmental sector have an opportunity to accumulate funds through bribery and other forms of corruption and to funnel them into the private sector, perhaps through relatives. Soon, the Soviet scholars fear, the officials stop supporting socialism and begin to form a capitalist class, with all its characteristic attitudes."[5] Such reflections mark a more cautious trend in Soviet thinking, which will have important consequences for the Middle East.

3. Consolidation of the communist states: The shift away from reliance on Left-wing nationalism has been complemented by a greater determination to build up the bloc of countries that are seen as being ruled by pro-Soviet parties. One important factor behind this has been the failure of the "non-capitalist road" as a means of achieving permanent alliances in the Third World. Another has been the threat posed by China, and the need felt by Moscow to maintain the loyalty of Third World communist states in the face of appeals from Peking. For states of this kind, full Soviet military support can be expected, and it is this which Cuba, Vietnam and South Yemen have enjoyed. It is also this factor which may go a long way to explaining the Soviet commitment to Afghanistan: the government in Kabul, despite its claims to the contrary, was that of an orthodox pro-Soviet communist party from April 1978 onwards and was treated as such in the protocol-conscious Soviet press. Such aid was on a quite different level from that given Nasserite Egypt or Baathist Iraq. The ability to honor such commitments was, obviously, enhanced by the first of three changes already mentioned, the increased military power of the Soviet Union. Indeed, too much attention is paid in the West to the individual personalities of the top Politburo members; too little to the diffuse shifts in generational attitude consequent upon the attainment by the U.S.S.R. of its new strategic strength. It is this latter factor, rather than the outcome of a factional or personal dispute, which marks present and future Soviet leaders off from their more cautious or adventurist predecessors. Their ability and determination to defend the fully-qualified members of their system is central to their present world view.

These, therefore, are the general contours of contemporary Soviet foreign policy. Some have been permanent features of Soviet practice for decades, but others reflect the changes of the 1970s, particularly an increased strategic capacity and a less sanguine view of Third World nationalist governments. While these contours delineate Soviet policy throughout the Third World, they are especially visible in the Middle East. This is the region nearest the Soviet Union, the one that has offered some of the greatest opportunities, and also the one that has given the Russians the greatest headaches.

III.

"THE UNCONTROLLABLE CENTER"

In Chapter II, we discussed the general lines of Soviet foreign policy, its evolution in the 1970s, and the overall Soviet "perception" of the Middle East region. The countries to the South of the U.S.S.R. constitute, as we have seen, a special concern because of the political risks involved, and their geographical location. The purpose of this chapter is to explore this "perception" in more detail, by considering how the U.S.S.R.'s leaders—peering Southwards from the Kremlin—view what can be called "the uncontrollable center."

Strategic Importance: Frontiers, Aid, Volatility

The Middle East, seen as that area stretching from Turkey to Afghanistan and including the whole of the Arab world, occupies a particular place in the Soviet view of the world for three reasons:

1. Frontiers: The Middle East borders the Soviet Union, and is indeed the only place, apart from the Russian-Finnish and Russian-Norwegian borders, where the U.S.S.R. physically adjoins the non-communist world. It is also the only place, other than the U.S.-Mexican border, where the industrialized and developing worlds meet directly. Viewed from the Kremlin, the U.S.S.R. has a belt of Warsaw Pact allies on the West, and China—hostile but under a considerable degree of central control—on the East. In between lies a central belt where no such strategic certainty exists: a line running over three thousand miles along the Black Sea, the Turkish and Iranian frontiers, and then across the Afghan plains to the knot of the Pamirs, a cartographer's conceit constructed by British officials in

the nineteenth century, where Russia, China, and Afghanistan all meet. What the West sees as the "northern tier" is, for the Russians, the southern tier, a line of countries whose international and internal orientations are of prime concern to them, just as much as the politics of the Caribbean and Central American countries are to the United States. Vaulting over these countries to the south, there are the Arab states with which Moscow has enjoyed closer relations over the past two decades, but which are strategically of secondary importance to the northern/southern tier.

The Middle East as a whole is by far the most volatile and exposed of the three major land flanks that the U.S.S.R. faces, and it is the one where the West has been most active in consolidating its own positions, ever since the Truman (1947) and Eisenhower (1957) Doctrines. Although not specifically designed for the area, the Nixon Doctrine (1969) found its most potent implementation there, in the arming of the Shah and the Saudis, and the Carter Doctrine (1980) was specifically concerned with the Persian Gulf. In both previous world wars this southern tier was the site of Russian military campaigns: there can be little doubt that this would be so in the event of a third global conflagration. The West sees this region as, at the moment, vital to its interests because of oil, but this is a passing concern, unlikely to last more than two or three decades more; for the Russians, this is a geographical reality that they must confront forever.

2. *Economic and military aid:* The scale of the Soviet commitment to the Middle East, in economic and military terms, has outstripped that to any other part of the non-communist world. The economic commitment has resulted from geographical proximity and the availability of energy supplies, and has focused on the northern tier (Iran, Afghanistan) and on Iraq. The military commitment has resulted from the Arab-Israeli dispute and has focused on the confrontation states (Egypt, Syria). This military presence is often cast as representing a primeval Russian quest for warm water ports. But while strictly naval considerations must play some part in Soviet policy, the main reasons why this military commitment has come about are: (i) the demands of the frontline states for high-level military technology; and (ii) the refusal of Western powers to arm the Arabs at any level comparable to the arms provided for Israel.

Figures for Soviet aid and trade show the special place that the Middle East occupies in Moscow's calculations: although Soviet aid and trade with the Third World are much lower than for comparable Western countries, the Middle East states do represent a significant proportion of overall Soviet involvement in the Third World. (Less than 10 percent of Soviet imports come from non-communist Third World countries, and the Soviet share of Third World exports, including oil, was 2.2 percent in 1976, compared with 28.5 percent for the EEC and 20.6 percent for the U.S. But well over half of this Soviet trade and aid policy is tied to the Middle Eastern area.) Of the ten major non-communist recipients of Soviet economic aid in the 1954-1976 period, no less than seven were in the Middle East: Turkey, Afghanistan, Egypt, Algeria, Iran, Iraq, and Syria. Of the ten Third World countries with the most trade with the U.S.S.R. in 1976, six were in the Middle East: Iraq, Egypt, Iran, Syria, Algeria, Afghanistan.[1] Estimates of Soviet military exports indicate that up to two-thirds of all post-war supplies to non-communist countries have gone to Middle East countries; in the 1971-1976 period, 60 percent went to just three countries: Egypt, Syria, and Iraq. The Soviet military presence in Egypt in the early 1970s was the largest ever outside the communist world (i.e., prior to Afghanistan), with around 25,000 personnel, berthing rights in Alexandria, and the use of six airfields. Of twenty-three non-communist countries identified as having received 60 percent or more of their equipment from the Soviet Union in the 1967-1976 period, nine are Arab League countries. Put another way, nine out of twenty-one Arab League states are, or have recently been, reliant on the U.S.S.R. for the bulk of their military supplies.[2]

Even the decline of arms transfers to Egypt has failed to break the pattern. In 1977 and 1978 Soviet arms supplies to the Third World accounted for around 25 percent of the world total, a higher percentage than was previously the case. The Middle East and North African countries figured prominently in this trade, with Ethiopia coming into prominence as a major recipient for the first time. Of total sales in 1977-78, Ethiopia accounted for about 30 percent of the total; four longer-term customers—Libya, Algeria, Syria, and India—accounted for another 55 percent; and among the twenty-two other countries acquiring Soviet weapons were South Yemen, Iraq, and Afghanistan.[3] Such a large commitment has, however, been a mixed experience for the Russians. It has provided a testing ground for Soviet equipment (especially in the 1973 Arab-Israeli war) and has given the opportunity for some major Soviet airlifts (Egypt in 1973, Ethiopia in 1977). But it has also involved a heavy commitment of Soviet prestige in dealing with countries which it has not been able to control. Of its present close allies, the only one that could, in any serious sense, be said to have a political system analogous to the Soviet Union's is South Yemen, and even here the similarity is debatable. In Ethiopia the officer corps has not been changed since the days of the Emperor. In Iraq the ruling Baath Party began executing and imprisoning communists in 1978. In Afghanistan the Russians have not had to take drastic and risky measures to protect their previously established position. In Sudan an adventurist coup attempt by Left-wing officers in July 1971 led to a bloody setback for Soviet influence.

The proportional scale of this Soviet involvement also needs to be offset by some mention of its absolute limits. First, as already mentioned, external trade in general and trade links with the Third World in particular, play a much less important role in the Soviet economic system than they do in that of the West. Moreover, whether or not one argues that the U.S.S.R. is a "socialist" country in any precise sense of that word, it is clear that its relations with the Third World are determined by different domestic forces from those operating in the West. There are not within the Soviet system private entities like the multinational corporations, the banks and the arms manufacturers of the West which exert pressure upon the executive branch to advance their commercial interests abroad. Indeed profit as a motive seems to play a secondary role: the Soviet trading negotiators certainly strive to win the best terms possible in their deals with Third World countries, and are hard bargainers. But, as we shall see later (Chapter IV), the overall balance of Soviet economic ventures in the Middle East would appear to have been deficient.

39

A second problem is that the provision of arms and economic aid has not proven to be any guarantee of lasting political influence in the countries concerned. If there are strings attached, they seem to be ones that give the supposed puppets an independent capacity, including the ability to break the strings themselves. Russian arms supplies to Egypt, Somalia, and Iraq have not kept their governments in line, and even Syria was able to invade Lebanon against Soviet protests in 1976. Indeed, a "socialist" orientation in internal policy has been an extremely uncertain factor in determining relations with the Soviet Union: the much earlier examples of Yugoslavia and China showed this to be the case, and the crisis in Afghanistan in late 1979 was caused by the fact that then President Hafizullah Amin was determined to defy Soviet advice and pressure, even though his regime depended on the U.S.S.R. for its very survival. One of the Soviet Union's longest-standing and most substantial partners in the Third World, both in economic and military terms, has been a country that espouses free enterprise and a Western democratic system, namely India. It has proven to be a much more viable partner than all the "Arab socialist" and sundry other radical nationalist regimes that the Soviet Union has been alleged at one time or another to be manipulating. A significant proportion of Soviet economic aid for 1979 went to a NATO country, Turkey. Yet the Indian and Arab experiences together highlight another problem with Soviet economic aid, namely the limited economic resources at its disposal for foreign programs and the limited range of goods it can export, especially those to which the middle classes in these countries aspire.

Soviet aid focuses on state-to-state, bilateral projects, usually in the heavy industrial sector. For example, nearly 80 percent of Soviet credits to Egypt were for hydroelectric and heavy industrial projects; the first major aid project outside the communist bloc was for an iron and steel complex at Bhilai, in India. While these are important ventures, they leave the door open for Western domination of many other economic sectors and ones that have greater popular impact. Even those countries such as Iraq that have nationalized considerable sectors of their own industry and imposed state control of foreign trade, and which

40

have signed friendship treaties with the Soviet Union, continue to do most of their trading with capitalist countries: for every Lada (Soviet-made Fiat) on the streets of Baghdad, there are several Italian Fiats, Volkswagens, or Citroens. Indeed, the pattern of Soviet relations over the past two decades with its closer partners in the non-communist Third world is marked by a striking asymmetry: the establishment of preponderant military links between those states and the Soviet Union, combined with the maintenance of much more diversified economic ones. The only non-communist Third World country that in the 1955-1975 period went to the Soviet Union for the majority of its economic as well as military contacts was the one most far removed from the Soviet image of a progressive Third World state: it was a conservative monarchy called Afghanistan.

3. Political volatility: The flow of Soviet arms is related to another factor which Moscow has shown acute awareness of, namely, that conflict between their respective clients in the Middle East and surrounding areas could lead to a war between the superpowers. The investment of prestige by both sides is considerable, and the strategic importance is even more so, for different reasons on either side (oil for the West, geography for the Russians). Both parties have acted through local allies they do not fully control, and the rationale advanced by both Moscow and Washington—that military supplies are needed to help keep the peace—obviously contains a high risk of a conflict exploding nonetheless. The Western claim has usually been that Soviet arms supplies to the region have been adventurist and inflammatory; yet the level of Soviet supplies has been less than that of the West. In the most dangerous confrontation of all, the Arab-Israeli one, the record shows that Soviet supplies have been consistently held at a level that would enable the Arabs to match Israel but not overwhelm it.[4] The dispatch of Soviet personnel to Egypt in the late 1960s was designed to halt Israeli penetration raids into Egypt and was intended to give the Russians more restraining control over the humiliated and potentially rash Egyptian forces.

In a range of other conflicts the Soviet Union has also

acted to prevent the situation from going out of control. In the Iraq-Iran border conflict of the late 1960s, the Soviet Union adopted a neutral stance, even though at that time Iraq was as clearly its local ally as Iran was Washington's. When Iran seized three Arab islands in the Gulf in November 1971, the Russians did not join the denunciations of this by its Arab allies. In the Ethiopian-Somali conflict of 1977-78, the Soviet Union tried to prevent a conflagration by urging conciliation via visits by former Soviet President Podgorny and Fidel Castro; while later sending large quantities of arms to support Ethiopia against an all-out Somali invasion attempt, the Russians made sure that no substantial crossings of the border by Ethiopian forces occurred. In February 1979, the Russians held back their ally South Yemen when it was in an advantageous position in its conflict with North Yemen, the latter backed by Saudi Arabia. Soviet policy over Afghanistan has also exemplified this: despite much Western speculation about "hot pursuit" raids into Pakistan by Afghan and/or Russian forces after December 1979, or about possible Soviet backing for covert Baluch and Pathan activities inside Pakistan, there was no evidence of any concerted Soviet thrust against the Pakistani government. Rather, Russia has made an attempt to contain the conflict within Afghanistan and thereby encourage Pakistan to diminish or even cease its backing to the Afghan rebels.

Soviet policy during the Iranian revolution has reflected similar fears of a great power confrontation: during the last weeks of the Shah's regime, in November 1978, Brezhnev warned the Americans not to intervene. In their response to the hostages issue, the Russians were primarily concerned with preventing a situation of direct superpower confrontation from developing (as were the Americans, who repeatedly pointed out that their operations against Iran were not "directed against" any third party). The Russian commentaries on Iran therefore laid primary stress upon non-interference by the United States and the need for a peaceful solution. While supporting release of the hostages, and while conversely making the occasional general statement of support for Iran, the dominant theme of Soviet commentary remained the need to avoid an armed conflict between the United States and Iran into which the U.S.S.R. might be drawn.

The Internal Impact: Minorities, Oil, Leadership Divisions

The Middle East has importance of another kind for the Soviet Union, namely that alone of the areas of the Third World, or indeed of the non-communist world, it has had a significant effect on the economic and political situation within Russia itself.

1. Muslim minorities: The potential threat to the Soviet regime posed by the minorities of Central Asia has been much discussed in recent years, and has become the subject of considerable wishful thinking in the West.[5] While probably exaggerated, the growth of Central Asian sentiment as a future destabilizing tendency should not be discounted altogether, and complements the rise of national and religious feeling in the Ukraine and Baltic states. The demographic facts are clear enough: of the 262 million population in the 1979 census, Russians make up half and Slavs two-thirds of the total. But the birth rates in the non-Slav republics are much higher. The population growth rate for the European U.S.S.R. in the 1970-79 period was 9 percent, compared to Tadjikistan 31 percent, Uzbekistan 30 percent, Armenia 22 percent, etc. *If* these trends continue, then at some point in the next century these non-Slav minorities will form a majority of the U.S.S.R.'s population. This development naturally raises the possibility of a revival of nationalistic and Islamic sentiment amongst these peoples, influenced by trends across the border in the Middle East.

Details on opposition activity are scarce, but there are signs of a new militancy among the Muslims of Central Asia. The underground Sufi religious sects, the Naqshbandi and the Qadyri, with contacts in Turkey and Iran, are said to maintain some contacts with co-believers across the border. The report to the 26th Congress of the C.P.S.U. from Turkmenistan reported on unspecified opposition by local mullahs.[6] Although the number of mosques is only around two hundred (compared with eight thousand at the end of the war) the majority of the population retains some religious belief, as evidenced by observation of festivals, endogenous marriage, and a refusal to use abortion (the **43** most common form of Soviet birth control). However, the coherence of this phenomenon should not be exaggerated. Not all of the non-Russian minorities are Muslims: the Christian Armenians and Georgians may be anti-Russian, but they are not going to align themselves with any new militant Islam. Even within the Muslim community there are sharp rivalries. As is so often the case, there is no one who distrusts a minority so much as another minority. Moreover, as Zhores Medvedev has pointed out, the very numerical extent of the minority groups (more than ninety) makes it much more difficult for them to pose a threat to the Slavs at the top.[7] The growth of distinct national entities— Uzbek, Kazakh, etc.—since 1917 has also eroded the grounds for a single pan-Islamic sentiment; for the example of the Iranian revolution makes clear that there is more that divides Muslims in a nationalistic era than unites them. The expectation that events in Afghanistan would arouse Muslim sentiment in the U.S.S.R. is not confirmed by firsthand observation: if anything, reports from Soviet Central Asia suggest support for the Soviet role.[8]

Two other points need to be made here. The first is that for many of these minorities the cultural rights are broader, and the standard of living is higher on the Russian than on the Middle Eastern side of the border; this is true for the Azerbaijanis and Turcomans, for example, who span the U.S.S.R.-Iranian border with Iran and Afghanistan. The death rate in Soviet Turkmenia in the mid-1970s was 7.2 per thousand, the number of doctors 2.7 per thousand, and the number of hospital beds 10.2 per thousand. In Afghanistan the average figures were 23.8 per thousand, 7.5 per thousand, and 0.2 per thousand respectively.[9] Literacy in Soviet Tadjikistan, where the population speaks a dialect of Persian, has gone from 2 percent to 99 percent under Soviet rule. Literacy in Iran is 30 percent, and in Afghanistan it is 10 percent. The higher levels of education in the Soviet areas are important not just in social welfare terms but also in undermining the appeals of a populist Islam of the kind that finds its greatest appeal among uneducated or semi-educated people in the Middle East.

Another salient distinction is that, despite its own self-image, the Islamic revival in the Middle East is not a purely spiritual trend: it rests upon specific religious traditions and identifiable social support. The Iranian movement was based on the Shia Muslim traditions and institutions of Persian towns which had survived and even expanded under the Pahlavi regime. Eighty percent of Soviet Muslims are Sunni Muslims, who do not have such institutions; moreover, independent commercial and religious institutions of the Iranian kind simply do not exist in the U.S.S.R. Nor could an Afghan-type movement get under way in which Sunni tribal forces challenged the central government: armed and semi-autonomous tribal groupings have been absent in Soviet Central Asia since the 1930s. Indeed, the pattern of Muslim resistance, insofar as this can be discerned, seems to be much more one of infiltration and accommodation within the central state, as Sunnis in other countries have done, rather than one of an independent challenge, along Shia Muslim lines. In Soviet Central Asia, the local populations have tried to gain influence within state and party and thereby to turn them to their advantage—sometimes, if official reports are anything to go by, in rather corrupt ways. And this implies that members of the Central Asian minorities may gain influence at a future date within the U.S.S.R. without this necessarily leading to a greater autonomy or a centrifugal pattern in the provinces. It is, after all, worth remembering that for a number of years the Soviet Union was ruled by someone from a minority nationality, namely Joseph Stalin; and the evidence does not suggest that Moscow showed greater indulgence towards the non-Russian republics during his period in office. No one can predict the future trends among the nationalities in the U.S.S.R.; but neither available evidence nor analysis of the objective situation suggest that concern about an opposition in the Muslim areas is a major factor in Soviet calculations.

2. Soviet Jewry: Another, countervailing, nationality factor that has implications for the Middle East is the presence within the U.S.S.R. of a militant Jewish minority, reflecting the persistence of anti-semitic sentiment in wide sections of Soviet society. This Jewish community has not acted as a "lobby" on the U.S. model; but its activities have had their impact on Soviet policy, since by seeking to meet U.S. congressional criticism by permitting Jewish emigra- **45**

tion, Moscow has created some new problems for itself in the Middle East. Through its international contacts, the Soviet Jewish community has made the emigration issue a domestic U.S. concern. Thus, despite the frequently hostile character of the Soviet society around them, the Jews constitute a calculation in Soviet policy on the Middle East. Although the decision to allow Jewish emigration has cost the Russians some legitimacy in Arab eyes, it was taken largely in response to the pressure from the U.S. Congress which, through the Jackson-Vanik Amendment of 1974, linked further U.S.-Soviet economic collaboration to the right of Soviet Jews to emigrate. Since that time, a considerable flow of Jewish emigration has come from the Soviet Union—around 260,000 exit visas were granted between 1974 and 1980.

This emigration has caused difficulties for the Soviet Union in the Arab world where, given the high educational level of many such emigrants, it is seen as a form of assistance to Israel. The impression of such assistance is increased by the fact that, for their different reasons, neither the Arabs nor the Israelis draw too much attention to the fact that less than half the Jewish emigrants who leave the Soviet Union actually go to Israel, the majority preferring Canada and the United States.[10] Hence while there is no Jewish lobby in the U.S.S.R. in the sense of a pressure that would directly inflect Soviet policy on the Arab-Israeli question, the presence of a militant Jewish community has, via the combination of internal and external pressures, so inflected Soviet policy that Moscow has made concessions that do affect the Soviet image in the Muslim world.

3. *Soviet oil:* The Middle East impinges on the Soviet economy more than any other Third World area; even if this is, so far, much less than is the case for advanced capitalist countries, it is not a negligible factor. The Soviet Union is the largest oil producer in the world, and accounts for around one-fifth of total world output; with net output in 1979 at 11.87 million barrels a day—outstripping consumption at 8.93 million barrels a day—it remains a net exporter.[11] But because of geographical factors it has benefitted the Soviet Union to import quantities of oil (from

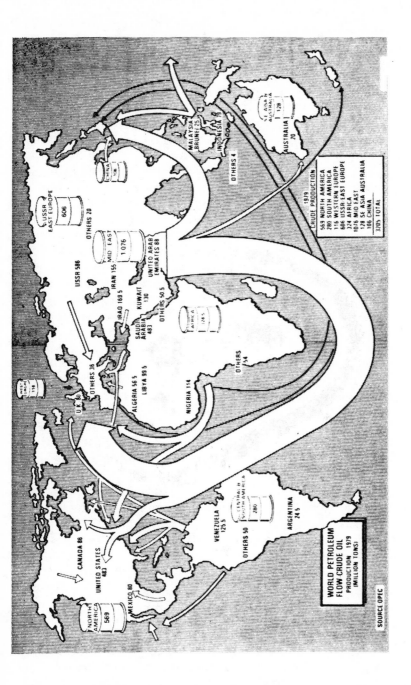

Iraq) and of gas (from Iran and Afghanistan), and thus to export more of its own production to European markets. This import policy has, however, placed strains on the Soviet economy. The rise in Middle Eastern oil and gas prices has forced the Russians to increase their payments to these countries. The revolution in Iran not only stopped work on a major new gas pipeline, IGAT-II from southern Iran to the U.S.S.R., but also cut off gas supplies already flowing from Iran to large areas of the Caucasus during the winter of 1978-79, thereby causing serious hardship in that region. However, the effects of Middle East price rises have, overall, been beneficial to the Soviet Union. Like other oil exporters who are not in OPEC (Mexico, Oman, Britain), it has followed OPEC pricing policies without being directly involved in price-rise decisions, or having to comply with boycotts. Indeed it was the OPEC price rises of 1973 which made it more profitable for the Russians to exploit Siberian fields, just as these rises made it viable for Western oil companies to develop the North Sea and Canada's Alberta province.

The U.S.S.R. faces a major foreign exchange problem: its manufactured goods are not of sufficient quality to compete on the world market, and it has had to rely on raw materials to make up its hard currency income. So, Soviet earnings from the sale of energy to Western Europe are especially important: at $6.7 billion in 1977 they made up half of all its hard currency earnings. Indeed Russia earns more from oil exports than do some OPEC states. Russia has also renegotiated its terms with Comecon countries: it has lowered the percentage of Comecon oil which it provides (65 percent in 1980), and has steadily raised prices so that by 1980 it was more or less half the OPEC rate, compared to a fraction thereof in 1975.

Considerable play is made of the fact that Soviet oil output is encountering new problems. The C.I.A. once predicted that Soviet oil output would peak at around 12 million barrels a day by the mid-1980s, and then begin a long-term decline. Given continuing increases in presumed Soviet demand, and in that of the Eastern European countries reliant on Soviet oil, this would necessitate the U.S.S.R. becoming a substantial oil importer, either on its own behalf or on behalf of the Comecon countries. The realization of this on the part of the Soviet leadership is regarded by many Western commentators as a cause, even *the* cause, of a Soviet drive to dominate the Gulf. This theme of an energy-starved U.S.S.R. is also echoed in right-wing Arab statements.

But there are a number of problems with this scenario. First of all, even though voiced by right-wing analysts, it is a curiously economistic explanation, reminiscent in many ways of vulgar Marxist explanations of American foreign policy in terms of a quest for raw materials and markets. It is pertinent to make the same reply to the vulgar Marxists of the Right as to those of the Left: that foreign policy is rarely reducible to simple economic concerns, and that access to raw materials is not always best guaranteed by the pursuit of political domination in those areas where the minerals or markets are to be found. Despite the neat reductionism of so much writing on the subject, the Soviet policy in Afghanistan bears no serious relationship to its oil policy. Moreover, the Russians must have learned from their dealings with countries like Iraq, and from observing the fate of Western dealings with OPEC, that in the contemporary world raw materials producers, especially producers of oil, have a measure of independence unknown in previous decades. On the basis of this recent experience, the Russians, if they needed Gulf oil, would be likely to keep their reliance on it to a medium level, precisely to avoid the vulnerability which excess reliance can bring about.

This still leaves open the question of how accurate the shortfall predictions are, whether phrased in terms of the C.I.A. reports or in the more general claim that the U.S.S.R. faces an "energy crisis" comparable to that of the West. The Russians clearly face a need to shift the main locations of their oil output, from west to east of the Urals, particularly to the Tyumen fields of Western Siberia. They also need to acquire new technology to open up Arctic and offshore resources; agreements concluded with Japanese firms, and with specialists in Alaskan output such as BP, illustrate this necessity. Furthermore, to make such efforts economically viable, they must continue to bring energy prices in the Soviet and Comecon economies up to or near those prevailing on the world markets. To a degree surprising in the secretive Soviet press these issues have been quite **49** widely debated in recent years: yet such relative openness may be a sign of confidence as much as of the panic that some foreign observers have detected in it. Although the Russians have admitted that their energy plans have not always been fulfilled (oil output in 1979 reportedly rose by only 2.4 percent, as opposed to the planned increase of 3.6 percent), such admissions are a long way from proving the C.I.A. case.

Indeed, the C.I.A. case has been called into question by the Agency itself—in one report (1977), it gave the expected mid-1980s shortfall as 3.5 million barrels a day, and later scaled this down to 600,000 barrels a day. Moreover, in May 1981, the C.I.A. announced that it no longer believed that the U.S.S.R. would have to import petroleum by the mid-1980s.[12] Independent experts have cast further doubt on the C.I.A.'s accuracy. A report published by the Economist Intelligence Unit in December 1980 calculated that Soviet oil and gas output would continue to rise through 1985, and that oil exports in 1990 would be in the range of 2.3 million barrels a day. The economist Marshall Goldman, Associate Director of the Russian Research Center at Harvard, believes that the C.I.A. calculations are based on "worst-case" scenarios which underestimate the Soviet capacity to take counter-measures, such as increased investment and conservation; Goldman's own prediction is that Moscow will take the necessary remedial measures to sustain output through 1985.[13]

The independent Swedish group Petro Studies predicts continued Soviet oil output at 12 million barrels a day through the 1980s, with a possible rise to 16 million barrels a day by 1990. It has drawn particular attention to a top-level decision taken in November 1979 to raise domestic Soviet prices from $2.75 a barrel—the level for fifteen years—to between $17 and $20, thereby enabling the oil industry to exploit new resources.[14] This pattern of "deregulation" is of course familiar from the U.S. energy situation, and, as in the United States, such price rises have the effect of bringing new sources of energy into play. It underlines the fact that the "energy crisis" is not so much an absolute problem—of a lack of energy resources—as it is a relative one, involving the cost of extraction; there is enough oil there for a much longer period, provided consumers are prepared to pay enough for it.

The British oil expert Peter Odell also queries the C.I.A. report; he draws attention to Soviet purchases of Western technology in 1978 and subsequent years as their way of solving production problems. He also argues that the C.I.A. report was designed primarily as a political act to scare U.S. public opinion into reducing its reliance on Middle East imports, and was only peripherally related to the situation inside the U.S.S.R. itself.[15] Indeed, compared to the majority of Western countries the U.S.S.R. is in a rather favorable energy situation. Its known reserves, at 71 billion barrels, made up 11 percent of the world total, and equal around seventeen times 1978 consumption. According to the OECD, it has an estimated 39 percent of all the world's gas reserves. The Russians claim—probably exaggeratedly, but indicative of a major reserve—to have 57 percent of the world's coal; they do account for 20 percent of world output. Moreover, they recently carried out a massive conservation campaign, and are building the equivalent of the Alaska pipeline every 4-5 weeks in order to get gas and oil out of Siberia. Unrestrained by environmentalist pressures, they are building up a nuclear energy industry that is scheduled to provide 33 percent of Comecon electricity by 1990. They certainly face hard choices in the energy area, but the available evidence does not suggest that they are in a dire situation either.

Indeed, whether or not the C.I.A. report was tinged by political concerns, it would seem likely that *other* political concerns have affected the interpretation of Soviet energy programs: the desire to find a neat and urgent reason for the Soviet Union's supposedly "forward" policy in the Arc of Crisis; the desire (which has roots within the oil industry going back to the 1920s), to keep the Russians out of the international market, whether as buyers or sellers—a desire rekindled by fears of new Soviet gas sales to Western Europe;[16] and the desire to feel that the Soviets are not exempt from the energy problems faced by the West.

Public discussion of the oil issue tends to coincide with a generalized modish tendency in the West to stress the economic problems facing the Soviet Union. Behind this perspective lie two political assumptions—either the belief that the U.S.S.R.'s internal problems can account for its **51** supposed "expansionism," or the belief that the Soviet Union will, because of its weaknesses, be vulnerable to certain forms of economic pressure from the West. The belief in Soviet vulnerability was a hallmark of the First Cold War: many expected that in the face of a commercial blockade and the recovery of Western Europe under the Marshall Plan, a war-devastated Russia would eventually have to give ground. It did not happen. Similar misconceptions underlay U.S. diplomacy in the 1970s—whether Kissinger's belief in the benefits of entangling Russia in commercial and banking arrangements, or Carter's hope that the grain embargo of 1980 and the ban on high technology exports would seriously alter Soviet policy in Afghanistan. Now it is true that the Soviet economy is inefficiently managed and has failed to realize anything like its full potential. It is also true that it faces problems of production and productivity in industry as well as agriculture, and that living standards are below those to which many Russians aspire. But nobody in the Soviet Union is starving, or sleeping on the streets: certain social services, such as public health (29.7 doctors per 1,000 population compared to 16.5 in North America), are in fact better for the mass of the population than those in North America. The Soviet economy is a long way from catastrophe and indeed it continues to expand at a sluggish rate at a time when the West has been in recession. Soviet GNP rose by 3.1 percent per year in the 1976-1979 period, and indications are that this kind of growth will continue.

The very nature of the Soviet social system also means that certain problems are less acutely felt: there are no raw material corporations, and no large numbers of private automobile owners to exert pressure on long-range energy planning. People are used to queuing. As Jerry Hough of Duke University has written: "For over sixty years Westerners have been talking about the difficulties in the Soviet economy, about the mistakes inherent in socialist planning, and, indeed, in the case of some analysts, about its imminent stagnation or even collapse. Yet in the broad historical perspective the Soviet economy has performed rather well, especially given its relative lack of foreign investment and the large proportion of its resources devoted to military purposes. The Soviet Union has moved from being a quite underdeveloped country to one capable of outstanding accomplishments in space. Its rate of economic growth, even in the "slowdown" of the 1970s, has been substantial, well above that of the United States. In the thirty-five years since the end of World War II, the consumer has enjoyed a steadily rising standard of living."[17]

Some proportion therefore needs to be introduced to counter the picture of an economically desperate and therefore expansionist or vulnerable Soviet Union. Apart from oil, the Soviet Union's international economic situation is by no means as dire as is often claimed. Russia has one enormous asset which it has used sparingly until now: it is the second largest producer of gold in the world. As with oil, the Soviet economy benefits from price rises in the world gold market which it has itself had to do little to bring about. The U.S.S.R. also produces large quantities of such strategic metals as manganese, cobalt, and chrome (for over 90 percent of which the United States has to rely on imports); it can also produce 6,000 tons of uranium annually. In human resources too it is quite well-placed, in particular through an educational system that turns out graduates with a much higher level of scientific qualification than is generally the case in the West. All in all, the economic condition of the Soviet Union is not so desperate as to force it to engage in rash gambles in the countries lying to its south. With its oil and gas, this region has been and will remain of importance to the Soviet economy, but this importance will more likely be mediated via normal commercial dealings rather than through the advance of the Red Army.[18]

4. Leadership divisions: The Middle East has been, on available evidence, a source of considerable dissension within the Soviet leadership, and, more generally, within the international commnist movement. Foreign issues such as Cuba, Czechoslovakia, and SALT negotiations also seem to have divided the Russian leadership, but no other Third World issue would seem to have so much factional effect. Again, geographical proximity and the unique scale of the Russian military involvement must go a long way to accounting for this. But so too must the very difficulty of predicting trends in this volatile region and the dangers of getting caught in regional crossfire. In Stalin's time there was, obviously enough, little room for dissension on this, as on other matters.*

Several disagreements have come into the open in more recent times, however. The falls of Foreign Minister Molotov in 1955 and of Marshal Zhukov in 1957 both came after they had adopted positions on the Arab world which diverged from the main line. Khrushchev alludes in his memoirs to people who opposed his collaboration with Cairo, calling them "narrow-minded skunks who raised such a stink and tried to poison the waters of our relationship with Egypt." One of the specific charges laid against Khrushchev at the time of his removal in October 1964 was that he had unjustifiably given the title Hero of the Soviet Union to Vice President Amer of Egypt.[20] While none of these leaders is thought to have fallen uniquely for these reasons, dissent over the Arab world seems to have played a part in their removals. From what appears to be a "hawkish" perspective, the Moscow City Party Secretary Nikolai Yegorychev was dismissed in 1967 for criticizing Brezhnev's failure to send troops to assist Egypt in the Six Day War.[21]

Between the third (1967) and fourth (1973) Arab-Israeli wars there seems to have been a major divergence within the Soviet Union between a group of military and defense experts, led by Marshal Gretchko, and a more strictly political group which included Brezhnev, Kosygin, and Podgorny. The military group is reported to have favored meeting Arab demands for more sophisticated weaponry, while the latter were more cautious: they were afraid of another 1967-style debacle, and they reflected the growing consensus amongst Soviet specialists on the region that

---

*Prior to Stalin's ascendancy, however, the accommodations reached with Enver Pasha in Turkey and Reza Khan in Iran were contested: the former was denounced by delegates to the October 1920 Congress of the then-dominant Independent Socialist Party, the U.S.P.D. in Germany, while the Comintern delegate Zinoviev was pleading with the German party to join the much smaller Communist Party. The latter agreement led to a revolt by sections of the Communist Party in Baku, capital of Soviet Azerbaijan, in late 1921, requiring disciplinary action by Lenin and his colleagues to check what they saw as an ultra-left outbreak.[19]

nationalist regimes like those in Egypt, Syria, Iraq, and Sudan were less reliable allies than earlier Khrushchevite doctrine had indicated. Studies of the Soviet press indicate clear and sustained differences of opinion on this matter and, on the basis of subsequent revelations by Egyptian sources, it seems that Cairo consciously played upon the divisions within the Soviet leadership in order to get the arms it wanted.[22]

More recently, the Middle East has again become an issue of dissension within and without the Soviet apparatus. The head of the Middle East section of the Foreign Ministry, Mikhail Sytenko, was reportedly dismissed early in 1979 for opposing a new attempt to open relations with Saudi Arabia. There was unconfirmed reports of dissent within the Politburo in the first part of 1979 over whether or not to send troops to Afghanistan, with the majority against intervention prevailing at that time. Reports that there was high level disagreement over the later, December 1979, dispatch of Soviet forces are, as yet, unsubstantiated, but the reported suicide of General Paputin, the man responsible for trying to alter the policy of Afghan President Hafizullah Amin just prior to his death, does indicate a degree of high tension within the Soviet military leadership.[23]

The Middle East has also been the source of considerable friction within the international communist movement. While this may have had little or no effect on actual Soviet policies, these Middle Eastern issues were significant as part of the wider disputes between the U.S.S.R. and its communist allies. As their dispute with the Soviet Union developed from the late 1950s onwards, the Chinese adopted different stands on the Middle East and implicitly criticized the Russians: they urged them to give more forthright backing to Syria in 1957, and they took up a more polemical tone after the U.S. invasion of Lebanon in July 1958. Peking also blamed the U.S.S.R. for the Israeli military successes in 1967, for not giving the Arabs enough support in 1973, and for the divisions over Camp David in 1978.[24] While claiming still to support the Palestinian movement, and blaming the Russians for abandoning this cause, the Chinese gave warm support to Sadat's policies and to his opening to Israel.

In a number of Eastern European countries positions divergent from those of the U.S.S.R. have been detected: the Yugoslavs, pressing a policy of Mediterranean non-alignment, were much more ardent supporters of the Algerian FLN and of Nasser than the Russians ever became; the Rumanians had closer ties with Israel, after their break with the Russians in the 1960s; and during the Czech Spring of 1968, there was open criticism by Prague dissidents of the Soviet policy of breaking diplomatic ties with Israel. Some Western European communist parties have also tended to be more sympathetic to Israel than is Moscow, and many were critical of Soviet support for the Ethiopian decision to crush the Eritrean resistance in 1978-1979. On Afghanistan, the Western parties divided into those critical of the Soviet intervention, led by the Italians, and those, like the French, who supported it. All these divergences must, in some measure, have added to the political risks that involvement in the region has forced the Russians to run.

The countries to the south are therefore of considerable importance to the Russians not just because of the opportunities for increased influence they may offer, but also because of their impact within the U.S.S.R. itself. The West's vulnerability because of oil is not matched on the Soviet side by any one such overriding concern, but it is equalled by the accumulation of concerns that we have identified. While the greatest Soviet involvement in the late 1970s has been in the Arc of Crisis countries, the focus of Soviet concern was for the two preceding decades on the Arab world, and in particular on Egypt. Analysis of this Russian-Arab connection, the subject of the next chapter, is therefore of considerable importance for understanding how the Russians approach this part of the world. It can show what their aims are. It can demonstrate what their weaknesses are. And it can identify some of the bitter lessons which were to inform the later policies in the four Arc countries, which are discussed in Part II.

IV:
THE ARAB WORLD: RISE AND FALL OF SOVIET INFLUENCE

The following chapter analyzes the record of Soviet policy in the Middle East. Neither from Moscow's point of view, nor from that of the Left opposition forces in the area, is it marked by great success. Yet, for that very reason, it may be a useful corrective to the present depiction of an overwhelming Russian political capacity in these countries.[1]

In the immediate aftermath of the Russian revolution, with the revolutionary wave blocked in Europe, the Bolsheviks saw the Middle East as a possible line of advance through which the world revolutionary movement could progress. While at first they supported the small communist forces in Iran and Turkey, they soon switched to the anti-imperialist nationalists in these countries. Through this shift, the Russians did not get revolutions in the Middle East, but they did obtain a *cordon sanitaire* in the epoch of "socialism in one country" that lasted until World War II. The nationalists quickly stamped out the communist forces. The ethnic and religious contiguity between Soviet and Middle Eastern areas, far from leading to some kind of revolutionary osmosis, as many had hoped, in fact compounded Russian difficulties by arousing anti-communist sentiment among Muslims south of the border. Elsewhere, in the Arab states, small communist nuclei developed, but nowhere was communism a leading force or able significantly to affect the course of events. In a comparative Third World perspective, politically and numerically, communism in the inter-war period was far weaker in the Middle East than in Latin America, let alone the Far East.

During World War II, Soviet troops invaded Iran (in August 1941) as part of a joint Anglo-Russian operation. This action was dictated by the fear that the then-ruler of Iran, Reza Shah, was sympathetic to Nazi Germany and by the desire to open a land corridor to Russia from the Persian

Gulf; subsequently, two-thirds of all Allied aid to Russia during World War II passed through Iran. Yet the occupation of northern Iran yielded Moscow no postwar strategic advantage. Iran became the first flashpoint of the Cold War, and the Russians conceded to the West: under U.S. pressure, the Russian troops were pulled out in 1946, leaving the U.S.-supported Iranian army and gendarmerie to crush the autonomous Left-wing republics of Kurdistan and Azerbaijan, and leaving a permanent residue of anti-Russian feeling in Iran. In 1948 the Soviet Union, which supported the partition of Palestine into two states, recognized Israel and, via Czechoslovakia, provided arms to the Zionist forces. In the early 1950s, they alienated the nationalist movement in Iran by initially casting Dr. Mosadeq as an American agent; and when Nasser first came to power in 1952, he was labelled a fascist in some communist literature on the region. Despite much emphasis in Washington on the "communist threat" to Iran in 1953, the pro-Soviet Tudeh Party did nothing to prevent the coup of that year. Stalin's sectarian policy towards nationalism, an unreconstructed inheritance from the early 1930s, therefore isolated the Soviet Union from the nationalist movement in the Middle East at this time.

Arab Nationalist Regimes

The breakthrough for Moscow came in 1955, when Nasser signed a major arms deal with the Czechs and, one year later, the Russians agreed to help in building the Aswan Dam after the West refused to provide any assistance. This agreement with Egypt paved the way for a series of other agreements over the next decade and a half with the self-proclaimed anti-imperialist regimes of the Arab world—Syria, Iraq, Algeria, Sudan, and Libya. Massive Soviet economic and military aid was provided. Meanwhile, after the Twentieth Congress of the C.P.S.U. in February 1956, official Soviet theory justified aid to these countries on the grounds that they were engaged in a "revolutionary democratic" transformation, a "non-capitalist" path of development that would eventually lead to socialism. Local communists were urged to cooperate with these nationalist military regimes. In Egypt, the communists dissolved their organization altogether in 1965, and merged with the Nasserite Arab Socialist Union. In other countries, Syria and Iraq, communists were urged by the Russians to join "united front" governments.

Yet despite the scale of Soviet aid and Moscow's indulgence towards regimes that were by no means communist, the relationships did not endure. After many years of Soviet quarrelling with Cairo, Sadat—who took over on Nasser's death in 1970—expelled most of the Russian forces in 1972, and in 1976 broke all cooperative links. Sadat also repudiated all of Egypt's debts to Russia. In Iraq and Sudan, communists who joined the governments were later ousted and in some cases killed. In Syria the communists had to accept a junior role in Baathist governments, and the party split under the pressure. In Algeria, after the initial euphoria of the Ben Bella years, the communists were driven underground. In Libya they were never a significant factor anyway.

The Russians were prepared to put up with problems of this kind over a number of years. Yet these disagreements did contradict the official theories about a new form of transition to socialism, the "non-capitalist road" through which left-wing nationalist states could lay the basis for socialism. The persecution of the local communists, and the transparently unequal "alliances" into which the communists were forced to enter, constituted one set of problems. But, over time, the Soviet Union's Arab allies went a stage further and openly renounced their ties with the U.S.S.R. The underlying reason was the social character of these regimes: nationalization and protectionism, far from encouraging a transition to socialism, were in fact building up local industry and finance within these states until they reached the point where they could more equally and actively integrate themselves into the capitalist system: in other words, the "non-capitalist road" was a stage in the development of *capitalism,* not, as the Soviet theoreticians supposed, of socialism. As in earlier cases, such as Ataturk's Turkey, the period of nationalist state control of the economy was followed by a more vigorous and pro-Western economic orientation. This has gone furthest in Egypt and Sudan, but trends in this direction are also evident in Iraq and Syria. The failure of the Soviet policy therefore rested not just on "misjudging Arab nationalism," but on misjudging what the class character of these regimes was, a class character that is necessary to explain the form that their nationalism took.[2]

One of the most controversial and important aspects of the Soviet record in the Arab countries has been the role of the communist parties. In Western eyes, and in the eyes of many Arab revolutionaries, Soviet patronage and influence were negative factors, since they pushed the communists into alliances that were deemed dangerous either to the West or to the Arab communists. In practice, however, the Arab communist parties proved of no real assistance in maintaining the Soviet position with Arab regimes, and indeed were a cause of dissent in these relations; and while the Russians certainly forced communists in Iraq and Egypt into such alliances, this Russian influence is not the main cause of the weakness of communist forces. Had the communists been stronger they could have defied the Russians and overthrown their nationalist allies—as they did in China. The weakness of communism in the Middle East cannot therefore be attributed primarily to Soviet mistakes. It must be attributed to the political character of the countries themselves, to the relatively opaque development of class consciousness, and to the vitality—exceptional in any comparative Third World perspective—of religious, ethnic and other sectarian differences.

The weakness of communism cannot, however, be seen as a simple historical given, a failure to overcome existing social problems; for where such movements did emerge, they were often met with repression. The first communists in Iran and Turkey were massacred in the early 1920s. The largest communist party in the Arab world, that of Iraq, had several hundred members killed when the Baath Party came to power in 1963.[3] The Sudanese party, the second largest in the Arab world, was decimated by the execution of its leaders in 1971 when an adventurist group of army officers tried to stage a Left-wing coup and provoked a Right-wing counter-attack against the Left as a whole. The weakness of the communist parties was therefore as much a cause as an effect of the difficulties which the Russians encountered in dealing with local nationalist governments.

These difficulties led the Russians to be rejected by so many Arab regimes in the way that they were.

The break with Egypt has been the most spectacular and the most damaging of such rejections. The shift towards de-statization and towards the West had begun under Nasser, but his death in October 1970 certainly accelerated the trend. Other factors helped to dislodge the Russians from their position: the conservative oil states were becoming more influential and they encouraged the denationalization of the economy and the swing to the West in international policies. At the same time, once Sadat had in some degree recouped the Arab position in the October 1973 war, he expelled the Russians and turned to Washington in the belief that the Americans, with—as he put it—99 percent of the cards in their hands, could put pressure on Israel in a way that the Russians could not. The latter, who had broken diplomatic relations with Israel in 1967, may now have regretted that they had left the field so open to Washington; certainly their lack of any formal access to Israel weakened Moscow's leverage in the region.[4]

At the start of the 1980s, Russian influence in the Middle East appears to be at a lower point than at any time since 1955. Egypt has broken all ties with Russia and has repudiated its $7 billion debt to Moscow. Sadat's hostility continues unabated, and he has repeatedly gone out of his way to insult the Russians. Moscow's most substantial economic and military ties were, until the late 1970s, with Iraq, yet here too the relationship is fraught. Since 1978 Iraq has been executing communists and is openly supplying Somalia and Eritrea with help against Soviet-supported Ethiopia. It has denounced the Soviet role in Afghanistan. Iraq exports about $500 million worth of oil to the Soviet Union and imports about $70 million worth of goods from the U.S.S.R.: a striking illustration of the asymmetry of military and economic links established by the U.S.S.R. with Third World countries. Russia's relations with Iraq worsened further after the Iranian revolution, when Moscow tried to establish a working relationship with Khomeini's regime, and when, after Iraq attacked Iran in September 1980, the Russians remained neutral.

Russia's relations with another ally of the 1960s had, by 1980, also taken a turn for the worse—namely, those with Algeria. The same asymmetry applied here as with Iraq: Algeria purchased military equipment from Russia but traded mainly with the West. The Algerians also resented Soviet neutrality in the dispute between Algeria and Morocco over the Western Sahara, while at the same time were seeking ways of establishing an independent and actively non-aligned position in the Third World. Algeria's role as mediator in the U.S.-Iranian hostages dispute was but one example of this independent foreign policy—and contrasted sharply with Moscow's opportunist handling of this issue, which involved backing the Iranians.

In the central Arab regions, the U.S.S.R. has maintained only two allies, Syria and Libya. At the start of the 1980s, there appeared to be some consolidation of relations with each. Syria signed a 20-year Treaty of Friendship and Cooperation with Moscow in 1980, and appeared, for the time being, to have reached an accommodation with the Russians which papered over their earlier disagreement over Syria's 1976 intervention in Lebanon. Libya, meanwhile, had come a long way since the early years of Qaddafi's regime, when the Tripoli press declared in red banner headlines that Russia was an "imperialist" country. Western sources spoke of up to $12 billion in Soviet arms sales to Libya, and hundreds of Soviet military technicians were reported in Libya, including some helping with advanced missiles.[5] Both these liaisons provoked some concern in the West, and seemed to betoken a sustained Soviet influence in the Arab heartlands. They also seemed to confirm an alarmist view of Soviet strategic intentions: Syria was increasingly in control of Lebanon, and remained the only front-line Arab state to be implacably hostile to Israel; while Libya's pro-Soviet orientation undermined the southern flank of NATO, and constituted a permanent challenge to Sadat's Egypt. Moreover, Libyan involvement in activities which, by any stretch of terminology, must be categorized as "terrorist" gave right-wing U.S. critics their opportunity to argue that Moscow was involved in orchestrating international terrorist activities through its "surrogates."

The value and reliability of these alliances was, however, considerably less than might at first glance appear to be the case. Taken together, these two alliances were no substitute for the one Russia had lost, namely that with Egypt. Whatever the Soviet military presence in Libya, it was far less than that which the Russians had had in Egypt in the early 1970s—with over 20,000 personnel deployed, and use of naval and air facilities. In both cases, moreover, the Soviet commitment was in part designed to check the tendency of both regimes towards reckless ventures which, if they had begun, might well have given greater advantage to the West: a Syrian miscalculation vis-a-vis Israel, or a Libyan one vis-a-vis Egypt could easily lead to disaster. Indeed, we cannot but suspect that one of the prime functions of the Soviet technicians in Libya is to prevent the Libyans from *using* the missiles they possess—just as Soviet personnel in Egypt in the late 1960s had had a similar role.

The treaty with Syria signed in 1980 appeared to signal a closer commitment, but neither side appeared too keen to put it to the test; and the many problems faced by Syria—Christian and Israeli opposition in Lebanon, a rising tide of Islamic fundamentalist militancy at home—were sure to keep the Damascus regime in a precarious condition. In Libya, Qaddafi's experiments with popular democracy and anti-bureaucratic struggle has produced little of substance: large oil revenues in a country with few people (3 million) enabled the regime to meet basic needs in housing and health. But the Libyan regime remains, over a decade after its establishment in the coup of 1969, a fragile entity, racked by factionalism and prone to erratic initiatives in domestic and foreign policy. Neither Syrian President Assad, nor Libyan President Qaddafi, are communists: indeed both are Arab nationalists, suspicious of communism, and capable of imprisoning or assassinating those left-wing opponents they feel are a threat. Their foreign policy initiatives are consistently taken for reasons of their own state interests, and not at the behest of Moscow. Time and again, divergences have arisen: in Syria's case over Lebanon, and in Libya's over Qaddafi's opposition to the Soviet role in Afghanistan and over the Libyan refusal to accept the legitimacy of an Israeli state. Qaddafi's visit to Moscow in April 1981 was the occasion for what were termed "frank exchanges," a polite euphemism for disagreements. The Soviet press censored his speech at the official banquet.[6]

Where Soviet influence has expanded is on the margins of the region: in the late 1970s, it enjoyed close relations with South Yemen. This country was carrying out a socialist transformation far more radical than any of the other allegedly "non-capitalist" states, and there was no apparent concession here to the particularities of "Arab socialism." Like Cuba and Angola, it was a government that grew out of a radical and non-communist movement which later became a more radical one. It provided refueling and crew replacement facilities to the Soviet Navy, and in 1979 it became an observer of Comecon and signed a Friendship Treaty with the U.S.S.R. However, its significance should not be overrated: it is a small (1.9 million inhabitants) and poor (average per capita income in 1978, $420) country, indeed the poorest in the Arab world. It is far removed geographically from the mainstream of Arab politics and unlikely to give the Russians any direct means of gaining political re-entry into the region as a whole. Moreover, the failure of the U.S.S.R. to provide adequate economic aid over time undermined the position which it had enjoyed in that country (see Chapter V).

A curious chapter in Soviet-Arab relations concerns Moscow's military links with North Yemen. Russia was the main provider of arms, via Egypt, to the Imam of Yemen in the 1950s, and to the republic that succeeded him in 1962. But when the North Yemeni government became more conservative in character and fell increasingly under Saudi influence in the 1970s, this link with Russia was almost terminated. The Saudis then promised to finance a switch by the Yemenis from Soviet to U.S. equipment, as they had helped to do in Egypt. In February 1979, a perfect opportunity to do so arose: small-scale fighting broke out between North and South Yemen, and then President Carter promised to supply North Yemen with nearly $400 million worth of U.S. military supplies, including F-5E fighters and M-60 tanks. The Saudis were to pay for this hardware, and a hundred Taiwanese pilots were to fly the planes until the Yemenis were able to do so. But this strategy was confounded when, in March, North and South Yemen made up their differences and signed an agreement to discuss unification of the two countries. The Saudis then blocked the supply of U.S. equipment, and the Russians promptly offered to sell the North Yemenis T-62 tanks and MiG-21 fighters. The Yemenis quickly accepted. Their officer corps, trained in Russian techniques and language, was reluctant to switch to U.S. materiel, and the Soviet financial terms were judged to be more attractive. The Saudi financing, meanwhile, signified increased dependence on that country. By year's end the Soviet military mission in North Yemen had risen to six hundred men, compared to a U.S. mission of around one hundred and a Saudi team estimated at thirty. By June 1980, the resident U.S. team had fallen to eight military advisors.[7]

There is an additional, and ironic, footnote to this North Yemeni episode. As the U.S. military attache in North Yemen at the time. Lt. Col. John Ruszkiewicz, was later to report, the intelligence estimates upon which U.S. policy had been based were false. Indeed, they were *falsified,* by Saudi and U.S. officials eager to invent a U.S.-Soviet confrontation that did not exist. According to Ruszkiewicz the reports sent to Washington on the 1979 Yemini conflict by the American Embassy in Sanaa (the North Yemeni capital) were "greatly exaggerated." When Ruskiewicz complained about this to higher authorities, he was told: "If Yemen had not happened at that particular time, it would have been invented." The military attache's conclusion is worth repeating, since it somewhat belies the official account of a Soviet "blueprint" for Middle East domination: "It seems to me we disastrously escalated our involvement in Vietnam as a result of an attack on an American warship in the Gulf of Tonkin which never occurred. I cannot help but view what happened in Yemen as a Middle East version of the Gulf of Tonkin incident."[8]

The Arab-Israeli Dispute

For the Arabs, the central issue in Middle Eastern politics remains the Arab-Israeli dispute. Here the Russians are in a difficult position. They have lost the influence they once had over Egypt and have been excluded from the negotiation process. Because of Saudi domination over the rejectionist camp, they are only on the sidelines as far as Sadat's opponents are concerned. They criticize U.S. policy, denounce Camp David, and call for a reconvening of the Geneva Conference. Some see the Soviet policy as a destructive and clearly "unhelpful" contribution to detente. The Chinese, who endorse Sadat, attribute the divisions in the Arab world to Soviet "trouble-making." However, closer analysis of this matter yields a rather different picture.[9]

First, the Russians do not oppose the existence of an Israeli state. They were among the first to recognize the state of Israel, and, although they broke diplomatic relations in 1967, they have never (in contrast to the Chinese) denied Israel's right to exist. They argue the only viable solution to be one that allows for the existence of both a Palestinian state and of Israel. They base their policy on U.N. Resolution 242 of 1967, and insist that Israel return to its 1967 boundaries. Throughout their relations with Arab states, they have never wavered on this point: they have, at the same time, never persuaded any Arab state to agree with them. As we shall see at the end of this chapter, the sustained divergence of the Soviets and the Arabs on this point is the basis upon which the Islamic delusion of a "Zionist-communist conspiracy" is built.

Second, Soviet arms supplies have never been such as to give the Arab states overall military superiority. They have been sufficient to give them the ability to resist Israeli attacks (in 1955, and again after 1967) or to launch a limited war (in 1973), the purpose of which was to reach a negotiated settlement. Some controversy surrounds the Soviet role in the 1973 war, when the Arabs launched a surprise attack: the Russians seem to have suspected that something was afoot, and they tried, obliquely, to warn the Americans of this; but there is no evidence that they planned or instigated the war, and their resupply and negotiation policies during it were designed to maintain the Arab position in the event of a cease-fire. Nor is there evidence that they seriously considered sending troops to the Middle East during this war (the supposed reason for Nixon's October 25 nuclear alert).[10] Soviet arms policy has always been governed by political considerations and correspondingly restricted: the Russians often quarreled with the Egyptians over arms supplies, and have done so more recently with Syria. To make an obvious point in this context: they have never acceded to Arab requests for nuclear weapons, despite the fact that Israel is known to have an almost immediate nuclear capacity.

Third, Soviet support for the Palestinians has been qualified and was slow to develop. Although the U.S.S.R. is on record as supporting the 1948 partition plan, it did not endorse the PLO when it was founded in 1964, unlike the Chinese. Official support came much more slowly. The first time Arafat visited Moscow he did so as part of Nasser's delegation in 1968; he had to hide inside the plane until the official ceremonies on the tarmac were over. Arafat's first two visits in his own right (February 1970, September 1971) were as a guest of the Soviet Afro-Asian Solidarity Organization, and he did not receive a state welcome from the Russians until July 1972. In the late 1960s, the dominant mood among Palestinians was extremely anti-Russian; the Soviets were seen as having betrayed the Arab cause and as refusing to assist the Palestinian movement. Nevertheless, while the Soviet press has always indicated official Soviet disapproval of terrorist actions—hijackings, the Munich massacre, etc.—relations with the PLO have improved and Moscow has become a champion of a Palestinian state, and a major arms supplier to the Palestinian movement. The Soviets have also encouraged a rapprochement between the PLO and the pro-Soviet communist party inside Isarel, Rakah. But they have continued to stress the need for Palestinian unity, and publicly to diverge from the Palestinians on the central issue of Israel's right to exist. They still do not accept the PLO as the *sole* representative of the Palestinian people. Even those sections of the PLO who support the establishment of a separate Palestinian state tend to see it as an intermediate step towards a final single entity, whereas Russia, basing itself on its 1948 position, envisages the two-state solution as permanent.

Fourth, while Soviet reaction to Camp David has been one of hostility, and while this is cast in the West as another sign of Soviet competitiveness at the expense of peace, the matter is somewhat more complicated than that. First of all, the Russians are opposed to step-by-step solutions, which they believe cannot work in the end. They say that Sadat's failure to achieve a comprehensive solution will, by provoking strong reactions, make it more difficult to reach a full agreement on the Palestinian question. Secondly, they believe that any solution negotiated by outside powers should be brought about bilaterally, by joint U.S.-Soviet negotiation. During the 1967 and 1973 wars, for example, they worked with Western diplomats to arrange for cease-fires. They were particularly enraged when the November 1977 initiatives by Sadat and the U.S. came within weeks of an important joint U.S.-Soviet declaration that they hoped would lead to a new bilateral initiative. One could take this a stage further: rather than their hostility to Camp David being against detente, part of the Soviet interpretation of detente is that mediation of this kind must be carried out through joint initiatives. This is necessary, they argue, to avoid one side using mediation for partisan purposes. They can hardly be accused of paranoia in this regard, since Kissinger made eminently clear that one of the aims of his diplomacy was precisely to seal the eviction of the Russians from the Middle East by arranging an Arab-Israeli settlement. His memoirs make clear just how Kissinger sought to manage this issue.[11] One could, moreover, compare this with cases where the Russians have attempted mediation: their negotiation between India and Pakistan, the Tashkent Summit of 1966, was not carried out in such a way as to dislodge the U.S. from its client in the dispute (Pakistan). And when the Russians tried to mediate between Ethiopia and Somalia in the spring of 1977, this cost them the friendship of a state that had previously been allied with them (Somalia). This latter case also reveals just how unhelpful Washington can be: Somalia's intransigence was, as will be shown below, encouraged by the Carter Administration.

Underlying these positions is an important difference in emphasis between the Soviet and Arab views of this question: while for the Arabs the Palestine issue is, at least officially, *the* central question in contemporary Middle Eastern politics, this is not so for the Russians. They see the balance of East-West relations and the protection of Russian security as more important than local disputes, however volatile or agonizing the latter may be. Indeed, below the surface of Russian commentary upon this question, it is possible to detect a note of irritation and even exasperation at the intransigent tone which the Arab states and the Palestinians have adopted on the question. Time and again, in official meetings, the Russian representatives have tried to persuade their Arab interlocutors to accept the principle of an Israeli state, and the Russian press has clearly condemned acts of terrorism by Palestinians. The initial Russian advance in the Arab world, the 1955 arms deal with Egypt, was designed not to enable Nasser to defeat Israel but to give support to Egypt and thereby undermine the Baghdad Pact which Dulles was establishing at that time. Soviet thinking on the Palestine question has certainly shifted somewhat since then, and now acknowledges the justice of the Palestinian cause itself, but the framework remains a broader one, of ensuring a just and lasting settlement of a dispute that could explode into a major world conflict, and in a region near the borders of the U.S.S.R. itself.

The results of this discord have been profound. Western commentators concerned about Soviet "expansionism" in the Arab world may tend to overlook the fact that in addition to their charges, there are two other critiques of Soviet policy which start from different positions altogether, namely those of the Middle Eastern Left, and of the militant Islamic Right.

For the Arab and Iranian Lefts, Russian policy in the Middle East has not been "expansionist," rather, it has not been active enough: Moscow has desisted from support of revolutionary movements in the region in order to consolidate relations with nationalist governments and to appease the imperialist countries. This critique began with the decision by Lenin and his associates to work with the nationalist governments of Turkey and Iran in 1921. It was greatly strengthened by Soviet support for military regimes in the 1950s and 1960s at the expense of local communists. Even where no Russian acceptance of the established power existed, Moscow has shown itself hesitant about supporting guerrilla movements—the Algerian FLN, the PLO, the Omani guerrillas, and now the Polisario Front of the Western Sahara. In the late 1960s especially, Russian policy was anathema throughout much of the Arab Left: Soviet "revisionism" was condemned for its hostility to guerrilla struggle. Whereas Soviet military and economic aid is seen in Western eyes as being used to guarantee political influence, the Left critique argues that this aid has **69** been too little and too exploitative.

As we have already seen in Chapter Three, the Chinese have engaged in a sustained propaganda campaign against Soviet policy in the Middle East, with the tone of this campaign varying in accordance with the current themes of Chinese foreign policy. In the 1960s, Peking's critique focused on what were supposedly Russian compromises and failures to adequately support the Arab and socially revolutionary causes. Since the early 1970s, however, Chinese criticism has focused on the opposite—Moscow's supposedly excessive interference in and hostility to legitimate governments. Whereas in the mid-1960s China was the more militant supporter of the PLO and accused Russia of collusion with the Shah, China is now praising Sadat's initiatives, and has attributed the Shah's fall to Soviet "subversion." This Chinese shift highlights what is in fact a reversal in their critique of the Soviet role: in the 1970s they claimed there was *too much* Soviet involvement in the region (a point shared with the Western picture); in the 1960s Soviet involvement was *too little* (a point shared with the Arab Left).[12]

The Islamic critique may at first sight appear to be less substantive than those of Western commentators or the Arab Left, but is probably the one that most people in the Middle East actually believe—itself a political fact of some importance. It is also not as totally ideological as might at first appear. This Islamic view, long propounded by the Saudis and now echoed in Iran, charges that the Soviet Union has withheld support for the "Arab" cause, and that this restraint has prevented the Arabs from clinching victory over Israel. It is a stock-in-trade of Sadat's rhetoric—as it once was of Qaddafi's. It serves to divert attention from what are often weaknesses within the Arab states themselves. But this critique of Russian policy goes on to argue that the U.S.S.R. has in fact been one of the forces *sustaining* Israel, a claim that draws on some potent if somewhat veiled racist themes within the Islamic worldview itself. The Arab states have not forgotten the important support given to the nascent state of Israel by Stalin in 1948; nor the fact that most of those who control Israel to this day were born in Eastern Europe ("the Pole Begin," etc.); nor that since 1967 the U.S.S.R. has allowed Jews to emigrate to Israel. Such emigration is seen as being a form of military support to Israel, given that many of the Jews involved have militarily usable skills and are of military service age. Not only the Saudis, but also Iraq and Libya raise this issue, and it serves to offset the impact of Soviet arms sales to the Arab world.

For the Saudis themselves and for Khomeini the matter does not, however, stop here. Much as this may surprise Senator Henry Jackson, it is widely held in the Arab world that Zionism is identical with, or related to, communism. For the core argument of the Islamic Right is simply that communism and Zionism are two heads of the same beast. The late King Feisal called on his people "to oppose all doctrines founded by the Zionists—the corrupt doctrines, the atheist communist doctrines which seek to deny the existence of God and to deviate from faith and from our Islamic religion." In a later interview, Feisal's successor, King Khaled, tells us: "We regard Zionism, communism and colonialism as a trinity allied against Arab and Islamic rights and aspirations. Our policy is based on that understanding, and it is natural for us to be always subjected to biased and poisonous campaigns at the hand of that very trinity."[13] The most base cliches of European fascism, linking communism and Jewry, can be found in the propaganda of this militant, and it must be emphasized, very widespread Islamic propaganda. Despite the fact that in 1926 the U.S.S.R. was the very first country in the world to recognize the Saudis as rulers of Arabia, and despite recent Soviet support for the widespread Arab rejection of Sadat, such is this Saudi hostility to Russia that to this day there are no diplomatic relations between Moscow and Riyadh. In Khomeini's Iran, Islamic rhetoric lashes out equally at Left and Right: the Jews in Palestine, the Ethiopian army in Eritrea, the revolutionary regime in Afghanistan—all are communist armies sent to attack Islam. From a supposedly more Left-wing stance, the Iraqi Baath Party has taken to discrediting its rival Communist Party by publicizing the latter's links to the "Zionist" Communist Party of Israel. If the West feels discomfited by its loss of influence over Arab states after Camp David, or over Iran, it should remember that these developments (combined with Afghanistan) have brought no rapproche- **71** ment between the countries concerned and the Soviet Union. Indeed these developments and the rise of militant Islamic forces have, if anything, only lowered Soviet influence still further by stealing from it even the possibility of championing anti-imperialist causes. We have seen the perverse result of this dilemma within which Soviet policy has been situated: the greatest defeat of U.S. policy in the Arab world was the rejection by the majority of Arab states of the Camp David agreement of 1978. Yet this setback for Washington brought little benefit to the U.S.S.R.: the conservative Arab states still declined to recognize Moscow, and the anti-American uproar throughout the Arab world coincided with a shift by one of Moscow's strongest allies, Iraq, into a more anti-communist stance. As Arab politicians railed against the Kha'en (or traitor) Sadat, and his capitulation to Washington, the firing squads were being lined up in Baghdad to execute members of the local pro-Soviet Communist Party.

A Net Deficit

The decline in Soviet influence within the Arab world has in some measure been offset by increased influence in some non-Arab states—Ethiopia, Afghanistan—and by a certain consolidation in the most peripheral of Arab states, South Yemen. This process will be addressed in Part Two, and has underlain the rise of the Arc of Crisis emergency for the West. In the Arab world, however, the Soviet record has been a negative and in many ways a disastrous one for the Russians, the exception of South Yemen not being enough to compensate in any way for the losses of Egypt, Somalia, Iraq, and Sudan. Despite its clear and more favorable stand on the Palestinian question, the U.S.S.R. has retained little influence on the diplomatic processes involved in Arab-Israeli negotiations. Yet, despite its weak hold on events, the Soviet Union now finds itself faced with a new American build-up in the Arab world precisely on the grounds that Soviet policy is supposed to be threatening the West's vital interests there.

Both Western and Soviet commentators have tended to see the Arab world in bipolar terms, viewing losses to their own side as gains to the other, and vice-versa. But this is not a zero-sum situation: the difficulties that the West has encountered in regard to the Arab world have not correlated with a commensurate rise in Soviet influence. Soviet expectations that nationalist and thereby anti-imperialist regimes would become reliable allies of theirs and potential converts to socialism have proven unfounded. In his encounters with Arab leaders, Nikita Khrushchev used to urge them to lay less stress on the supposed common bond of Arab brotherhood and more on class factors underlying the politics of the Middle East: "Arab nationalism is not the zenith of happiness," he once told a visiting Egyptian delegation led by Anwar Sadat. During a visit to Egypt in 1964, Khrushchev went even further in his attack upon the classless character of Arab unity slogans, by asking Egyptian trade unionists what they had in common with the Amir of Kuwait: "There is some little ruler sitting there, an Arab of course, a Muslim. He is giving bribes. He lives the life of the rich, but he is trading in the wealth of his people. He never had any conscience and he will never have any. Will you come to terms with him on unification? It is easier to eat three *puds* of salt than to reach an agreement with him, although you are both Arabs and Muslims."[14] In more delicate tones, Russian writers on the "non-capitalist road" have tried to stress the progressive class character behind Arab nationalism which, under proper guidance, could enable the Arab world to make a transition to socialism. But the turn of events has forced the Russians to reconsider their theories of the "non-capitalist road" and to look more skeptically at apparently radical nationalist regimes. If the West finds dealing with the Arab world difficult, it should not be forgotten how intractable and unrewarding the Russians have found it too.

The decline in Soviet influence in the main countries of the Arab world has, however, coincided with the dramatic increase in Soviet influence on the periphery—in Ethiopia, South Yemen, and Afghanistan—and with the fall of Western positions in Iran. As already noted, this process has coincided with the realization that the United States will for some years be very reliant upon supplies of oil from the Persian Gulf. It is in this context, one largely external to the Arab world as such, that the Arc of Crisis theory and allegations of an adventurist new Soviet foreign policy have arisen.

PART II:
THE ARC OF CRISIS

V:

THE FOUR CRISIS COUNTRIES: IRAN, AFGHANISTAN, SOUTH YEMEN, ETHIOPIA

As we have seen, the concept of the "Arc of Crisis" came into being towards the end of 1978 as the New Cold War gathered force. This image had its roots both in regional developments (a set of revolutionary upsurges along with advances in Soviet influence) and in factors intrinsic to the West itself (growing energy dependence, an upsurge in Russophobic attitudes). Within this generally alarmist perspective, there are variants of the arc theme: a strong version attributes all threatening developments to Soviet instigation, and a weaker one stresses Soviet "exploitation" of these developments, even where Moscow was not behind everything that occurred. Yet even exponents of this weaker version insist on Soviet "responsibility" for the larger pattern of instability, and stress the need for Western countermeasures. Kissinger is one such advocate, and successive Secretaries of Defense have advocated formation of the Rapid Deployment Force precisely on the grounds that it is needed to cope with "turbulence" that could open the way for Soviet advances. Secretary of State Haig's pursuit of a "strategic consensus" in the Middle East in early 1981 was a continuation of this process.

The logic of much of the "Arc" discussion is unsound: it involves a "deductivist" approach masquerading as an "inductivist" one, i.e., it pretends to prove its *general* case by using a set of specific examples. But what it is really doing is to interpret these examples in the light of an already accepted and unstated general theory: e.g., Soviet advances in South Yemen "prove" that Russia is an expansionist power trying to throttle the West's oil supplies. Yet, if one looks a little closer, it turns out that the events in South Yemen have been explicated on the basis of prior assumptions about what Soviet policy is. In the

77

discussion that follows, we will reject this ahistorical approach and attempt to discover what really occurred in Iran, Afghanistan, South Yemen and Ethiopia—the four Arc countries that are normally singled out as cases of Soviet instigation that justify a stronger Western response. A reconstruction of the record allows a rather different picture to emerge, one that contrasts not just with the simplistic alarmism of the hard-liners, but also with the somewhat more subtle perspective of a Kissinger. Since so much is supposedly "proven" by events in these four countries, such an investigation may clear away some misconceptions. It may also yield a quite distinct critique of Soviet policy.

Extrapolating from the variations and repetitions, the argument for a Western counter-offensive can be summarized under three headings:

1. External causation: During the late 1970s, a series of Asian and African regimes sympathetic to the West have been overthrown and/or regimes sympathetic to the Soviet Union have been established. This is, more or less, attributed to Soviet "interference." These developments are especially clear in four countries: Iran, Afghanistan, South Yemen, Ethiopia. Events in these countries must be seen primarily in terms of the strategic relationship between East and West, and as deliberate advances by the Soviet Union.

2. U.S. "innocence": The U.S. role in this has been an innocent one, based on unwarranted passivity and a misplaced commitment to non-involvement. Crippled by Congressional constraints on both covert and overt military action, and weighed down by a "post-Vietnam complex," the United States lost the initiative in this region in the late 1970s.

3. A Soviet "grand design": The Soviet Union is an expansionist power bent on implementing a "master plan" that goes back to Czarist times of breaking through to the Indian Ocean. Local forces are, wittingly or not, its clients or "surrogates" and acting at its behest. Although he qualifies his statements, Kissinger, as we have noted, argues in a similar way: "We simply do not understand that what happened in the Horn of Africa had a geopolitical design, independent of any specific action that the Soviet Union might have undertaken."

An alternative to this interpretation of the Soviet role in the Arc countries is an essential component of any reconstituted, balanced, analysis of the region.

1. Internal causation: Instead of arguing that the upheavals in these countries are primarily fostered from outside, it can be shown that in each of the four principal countries concerned, the fundamental changes were primarily due to the evolution of identifiable *internal* conflicts. The Soviet Union played no instigatory role in these evolutions. The similarity of the four countries is not due therefore to their common fate as victims of Soviet designs, but rather from the fact that in each, autonomous revolutionary processes have matured in such a way that the interests of the United States have been reduced.

2. U.S. instigation: Where there *was* an external catalyst, it came from the West or the West's allies. The U.S. responsibility in these situations, moreover, has been greater than the Rightist critics have conceded. In two of these states, Iran and Ethiopia, popular explosions had the ferocity they did partly because of long years of repression, for which the United States bears much responsibility. Furthermore, U.S. interference, directly or via U.S. junior allies, has remained a factor in the radicalization of each of the four countries concerned.

3. Soviet reactions: The Soviet Union certainly has taken advantage of these developments and plays an increasingly visible role, where the situation allows. But this is quite different from claiming that the Soviet Union has stage-managed events, or that it is somehow behaving as an "imperialist" power. It also overstates the degree of current Soviet control over these countries and the benefit that Moscow derives from its alliances with them.

Taking each of the four countries in turn, it is possible to give a summary account of the changed political situ- **79** ation from 1978 onwards, beginning with Iran.

Iran: A Populist Revolution

At the beginning of 1978, the active opposition to the Shah seemed to be confined to the urban middle class and to students, yet by mid-January these forces had been joined by the religious officials, the mullahs. They in turn mobilized the mass of urban poor in a series of street demonstrations from February onwards. By September, the Shah had to impose martial law, and by the end of the year, after three months of strikes, he had been persuaded to leave the country (at least temporarily) by the Carter Administration. This he did on January 16, 1979, and on February 10-11, a mass uprising installed Khomeini's followers in power.

The causes of this very deep-rooted and rapidly expanded popular movement are essentially three: first, a political revolt against twenty-five years of monarchical dictatorship; secondly, a social revolt against the increasing inequities and material problems associated with the pattern of capitalist development in Iran; and thirdly, a nationalist and Islamic revolt against the imposition of Western advisers and culture upon Iran, coupled with Iran's subservience to Washington in regional affairs. The causes of the movement were pre-eminently internal to Iran, and the one critical source of external instigation was the Ayatollah Khomeini, the Iranian religious leader whom the Shah had exiled in 1964. Some Western commentators have tried to claim that there was Soviet influence—either directly, or indirectly via Libya. Former C.I.A. director Richard Helms and British journalists Robert Moss and Lord Chalfont have tried their hand at this, and U.S. politicians have talked in vague terms about Soviet "interference" in Iran.[1] But this is untenable—not least because the Islamic movement in Iran is so anti-communist. There is no need to invoke outside influence to explain the spread and ferocity of the 1978-79 popular revolution in Iran. In so far as this revolution was partly caused by outside interference it was that of the United States—which sustained the Pahlavi monarchy for so long, and thereby provoked a nationalist counter-reaction.[2]

Events since the fall of the Shah have hardly confirmed the idea that it was all a communist conspiracy, or indeed that the pro-Soviet forces played a major role at all. The orientation of Iran's political leadership, and in particular that of the Ayatollah Khomeini, has been ferociously anti-communist. In a major speech on the occasion of the Persian New Year, on March 21, 1980, Khomeini denounced "the plunderers and occupiers of the aggressive East," and "the so-called supporters of the working class" who had seized Afghanistan. A month later, on April 28, he said that the government should show no leniency or forgiveness to the Leftist groups opposing him in Kurdistan. When I met Iranian Foreign Minister Ibrahim Yazdi in Tehran in August 1979, must of the interview consisted of a long denunciation of the supposed iniquities of Marxism and

communism. Hundreds of Leftists have been attacked, imprisoned, or killed by the Islamic Guards, with Khomeini's tacit agreement. Some Western writers have tried to make out that individual members of Khomeini's entourage, such as Sadegh Ghotbzadeh, Foreign Minister during the hostage crisis, are secretly Leftists; but this is unfounded speculation.[3] Indeed, it is Ghotbzedeh who had led Muslim attempts to coordinate support for the Afghan rebels, and who was then most denounced by the Russians and by Iranian communists. There was also considerable effort expended in the U.S. press in trying to establish that the students who seized the American hostages in Tehran in November 1979 were Leftists; but all available evidence shows decisively that they were Right-wing zealots, followers of the radical group of Dr. Peiman—the Movement of Muslim Strugglers—and that they resisted later attempts by Left-wingers to participate in the occupation of the American Embassy.[4]

Soviet policy toward Khomeini's government has been cautious. In keeping with its general abstentionist response to difficult issues, the Soviet press did not devote much coverage to Iran in 1979; it did welcome the nationalization measures and Iran's departure from CENTO, and it criticized the repression of the Kurds in August. The strongest criticism came late in 1979 in an article written by the senior commentator Alexander Bovin; but this aroused protests from the Iranian government and its content was not repeated.[5] Western critics often point to the case of the National Voice of Iran, a Persian-language program beamed from Baku in Soviet Azerbaijan which has been more outspokenly critical of the West than the Russian government; but while this radio is certainly an arm of the Soviet state, it has by all accounts a small audience in Iran itself and can hardly be held responsible for the course of events there.

Soviet policy on the hostages issue was inconsistent. The pro-Soviet forces inside Iran had nothing to do with the hostages' seizure, and soon after November 4 the Soviet Union made clear its position against hostage-taking, in the U.N. Security Council vote and in the International Court at The Hague. Visitors to the Soviet Union were assured that the Russians do not endorse such actions. Yet after the first weeks, the emphasis of Russian commentary seemed to change. This was as a result of: (a) the crisis over the intervention in Afghanistan which came six weeks later; and (b) the threat of direct U.S. action against Iran in connection with the seizure of the hostages. In this new context, the overriding concern of Soviet policy became that of preventing an American intervention in Iran, which would have faced the Russians with difficult and potentially humiliating choices. The second Soviet goal was to rally maximum sympathy to its own cause in order to head off Iranian hostility over Afghanistan. From the start of 1980, therefore, the Russians played down their criticism over the seizing of the hostages, even though the Iranian action represented a form of political practice that they would not endorse.

Soviet relations with Tehran improved somewhat in the latter part of 1980 following the Iraqi attack upon Iran. The Soviet Union remained neutral in this war, and repeated its view that military action could not solve disputes of this kind. In the light of the fact that Moscow had a treaty with Iraq, its neutrality could be seen as a "tilt" to Iran: yet too much should not be read into this. Moscow had taken up the same position during the previous spate of hostilities between the two countries, in 1969, at a time when the Shah was in power. The one area where some closer collaboration developed was in the economic field, and in early December 1980 the two countries agreed to increased trade; this was especially useful to Iran in the light of the Iraqi attacks on Iranian ports in the Gulf. Inside Iran, the pro-Soviet Tudeh Party appeared to enjoy an official indulgence not extended to other parties of the Left: it was able to publish its newspaper *Mardom* more or less unmolested, and it reciprocated by craven endorsement of the Islamic authorities. Yet this alliance was not all that substantial: Iranian officials continued to berate the Russians for their role in Afghanistan; Radio Iran began broadcasting agitatory programs to Soviet Central Asia; and no major military agreements were reached, despite Iran's need for arms in the face of the Iraqi attack. Nevertheless, the Russians were particularly sympathetic to Iranian positions in the last weeks of the hostage affair: they repeated Iranian claims that U.S. forces in the Gulf were about to invade Iran, and that the hostages had been brainwashed. It seems that the Propaganda Department of the Central Committee issued instructions to this effect, in order to win favor with the Iranians.[6]

This policy shift is, however, quite distinct from any direct Soviet influence on events in Iran, such influence remaining, by all accounts, singularly low. Overall, the Russians have made little contribution to the course of events in pre- and post-revolutionary Iran. While no one can say what will happen in the future, and while the turmoil of the Iranian revolution is probably still in its earlier stages, enough is known to be able to reject the claim that the Soviet Union, or pro-Soviet groups, played a substantial role in the overthrow of the Shah or in the affairs of the first republican government.

Afghanistan: Transformation from Above?

Afghanistan poses a different set of issues. Here it is necessary to separate discussion of the April 1978 coup, which brought a pro-Soviet government to power, from the events of December 1979, in which tens of thousands of Soviet troops entered the country.[7] Long before the Soviet intervention of 1979, it was common to hear Western commentators talking blithely in terms of a "Soviet-supported" coup. The coup in question, that of April 27, 1978, overthrew the government of President Mohammad Daud, which had itself come to power through a coup in July 1973. The April revolution installed a new regime headed by President Nur Mohammad Taraki. To all intents and purposes, this new Afghan regime was controlled by the People's Democratic Party of Afghanistan (P.D.P.A.), which had grown out of an underground communist group that had been established in 1965.

The PDPA was certainly pro-Moscow in orientation, and the Afghan Army has for the past twenty years or so been almost entirely equipped and trained by the Soviet Union. But does this mean that the Russians instigated the coup? No. Closer examination shows that the causes of the April events were, again, predominantly internal; the main outside influence was a Rightist one, namely from Iran.

Source: U.S. Department of State.

Daud had initially allied with part of the PDPA (it was split into two factions from 1967 to 1977) and had promised radical changes, such as land reform. But after 1974, and under increasing pressure from the Shah—by now playing his counter-revolutionary regional role—Daud abandoned his earlier promises. He broke with the P.D.P.A., reached economic agreements with the Shah that were generally felt in Afghanistan to be exploitative, abandoned Afghan

85

support for the Pushtun and Baluchi peoples in Pakistan, and allowed officials from SAVAK, Iran's secret police, to work within the Afghan state machine.

Meanwhile the economy of Afghanistan was deteriorating, with population rising faster than food output, unemployment over 20 percent, a million Afghan men forced to emigrate to find work, and the foreign debt mounting. Literacy was below 10 percent and per-capita income was $150 a year. By early 1978, a clash between Daud and the P.D.P.A. was inevitable; when Daud tried to arrest the P.D.P.A. leadership in early April, the party's underground organization, well-entrenched in the military but under the command of a civilian Central Committee member (Hafizullah Amin) struck back and seized power on April 27. Here again a more detailed study of what went on inside these countries reveals that *internal* factors were the main determinants; in so far as there was any outside pressure, it came from Iran.

The question of the Soviet role in the April 1978 coup may appear trivial in the light of what subsequently occurred. But it is not, precisely because it bears upon the question of whether or not Soviet policy is dictated by a deliberate expansionist thrust; and interpretation of the later Soviet intervention rests partly upon how the 1978 coup is viewed. A State Department official whom I interviewed in April 1979 made clear that in his view the person mainly responsible for the coup had been Daud himself, who brought about the fall of his own government by provoking the Left into a defensive reaction. This is borne out by the South Asian specialist Selig Harrison, who visited Kabul in 1977 and who was alarmed by what he saw as the Shah's destabilizing role. He found Foreign Ministry officials in Tehran who "spoke confidently of the leverage that SAVAK was exercising on the Daud regime," and he concluded: "Put in perspective, the 1978 Afghan coup emerges as one of the more disastrous legacies of the Shah's ambitious effort to roll back Soviet influence in surrounding countries and create a modern version of the ancient Persian Empire."[8] While Harrison argues that the Russians *might* have tried to react to the Shah's policies at some future date, he maintains, by a careful reconstruction of events, that the coup was an improvised response to the assassination of a leading communist and the subsequent arrest of much of the P.D.P.A. leadership.

Afghanistan was, long before this, a rather special case as far as Soviet policy in the region is concerned. Alone of the countries in the region, it was the one which Washington refused to aid substantially; the reason being that aid to Afghanistan would have antagonized a more important candidate for U.S. support, namely Pakistan. Consequently, and despite the fact that Afghanistan was an extremely conservative country dominated by a semi-feudal monarchy, it turned to Moscow for help and by the early 1960s relied on the U.S.S.R. for most of its trade and military assistance. Now, since the Soviet intervention of 1979 it has become conventional for Western commentators to talk of an underlying logic of Soviet "expansionism" in Afghanistan, going back to Czarist times; yet this is historically untenable, since Russian policy in Afghanistan was politically neutral throughout the postwar period, up to the 1978 crisis. Indeed it is worth quoting the words of one American expert, Marshall Goldman, whose assessment of Soviet assistance to Afghanistan at the end of the 1960s was as follows: "Soviet aid to Afghanistan has been immensely successful. The Russians have avoided most forms of political interference. Afghanistan has maintained its neutrality despite the nearness of its imposing neighbor and the remoteness of all forms of countervailing help. The Soviet Union has become Afghanistan's most important trading partner, in many cases out of choice, not compulsion. Russian aid projects on the whole have been well suited to Afghanistan's needs. Even American officials are hard pressed to find major flaws. It would be comforting to ascribe Russian success in Afghanistan to the proximity of the two countries, but this is not the complete answer. The record indicates that flexibility and determination to show that the Soviet Union can co-exist with a smaller nation have been of equal importance."[9]

The dramatic change of circumstances that took place in 1978 came therefore as a result not of Russian but of the Iranian interference, a clash between the incumbent President Daud and his Left-wing opposition led to the latter coming to power through a military coup. The Soviet Union agreed to provide additional economic and military assistance to the new regime, which was headed by pro-Soviet communists. But the level of Russian presence in Afghanistan only increased dramatically in mid-1979, when substantial rural resistance to the regime's reforms broke out. Later in that year, the Russians tried to help a faction inside the government to remove the most hated man in the regime, Premier Hafizullah Amin, and it was only in December that they managed to do so. Amin had so weakened the structures of party and state and so inflamed the tribal rebellion by his repression that the Russians decided they could only restabilize the situation by sending in thousands of their own troops. This move was dictated by the internal situation in Afghanistan, i.e. the deterioration of the new regime's condition. It was not, so far as can be determined, part of a broader aggressive design in the Middle East. Indeed, viewed in terms of Soviet interests in Southwest Asia as a whole, this move was counterproductive: it strengthened anti-communist sentiment in the Muslim world, especially Iran, and legitimized a new level of U.S. intervention under the "Carter Doctrine," proclaimed in January 1980.

Hence, contrary to the standard picture of Soviet policy presented by its American opponents, the evidence indicates that the Russians tried their best to avoid going into Afghanistan directly. Indeed, they consistently resisted requests from Taraki and Amin earlier in 1979 to do so. Moreover, it was a sign of how little the Russians actually controlled the situation inside the Afghan regime—even with their levels of advisers and aid—that they could not deflect Amin from his self-destructive policies and were forced to try and get rid of him. The subsequent problems that the Russians have encountered in Afghanistan hardly confirm the idea that their policy there since 1978 has been part of some pre-conceived plan, or part of some broader expansionist drive, or that the P.D.P.A. has proved to be a pliant servant. The Soviet intervention has had military benefits, but these were not a decisive motivation. If Taraki and Amin were indeed the "Soviet puppets" that so much Western analysis made them out to be, then the record of their periods in power becomes even more unintelligible than it might otherwise be: for it was the mistakes of Afghan communists which created the crisis into which the

Russians were reluctantly drawn.

To argue this is not to accept the account which the Russians give of the December 1979 events, according to which the Soviet forces were invited in by the Afghan government to assist it in countering an external aggression.[10] Part of this account is true—the available evidence suggests that Hafizullah Amin did invite the Russian troops, and that he imagined that the forces which began arriving on December 24 were there to bolster his regime.[11] Western use of the term "invasion" tends to obscure these facts. Moreover, elements of at least two Soviet divisions were already stationed in Afghanistan weeks prior to the late December invasion; this could only have been with the approval of Amin. Yet the Russian account is also untenable, for a number of reasons: (1) it omits the fact that the Russian forces, once they arrived, were used to replace Amin by the rival group led by Babrak Karmal; (2) it concocts a fantastic story according to which Amin was, in fact, a C.I.A. agent all along; (3) it exaggerates the level of external responsibility for the crisis in Afghanistan and thereby shifts blame from the P.D.P.A. and its Russian advisers whose repressive policies had, during the earlier months of 1979, done so much to antagonize the Afghan population. The fact that much of what Western sources have said about Afghanistan is untrue should not obscure the fact that the Russians have larded their tenuous case with lies of their own. The Russians appear not to have wanted to combine the introduction of their troops with the forcible removal of Amin; but it would seem that their plans went awry and that, after failing to remove Amin by political pressure, they were forced to impose a new leadership that was then sustained by the intervention force.[12]

There are several other aspects of the Afghanistan case and of its implications for Soviet policy in the region which need to be further considered. These will be examined later, in Chapter Seven. What concerns us here however, is the question of how far the changes in Afghanistan—the April 1978 coup and the December 1979 intervention—can be seen as the results of Soviet instigation and long-term intentions. The conclusion that emerges from the evidence is that neither of these two crises was the product of a deliberate Soviet initiative: the former reflected the explosion of internal tensions, aggravated by Iran; the latter was a Soviet response to its inability to influence the situation in Afghanistan, and the risks entailed by this turn of events.

South Yemen: Revolutionary Outpost in the Arabian Peninsula

South Yemen is frequently invoked as a country which the Soviet Union somehow seized control of through a coup in 1978. One cannot escape the impression that here, as with the case of the April 1978 Afghan events, a general public ignorance provides the conditions in which most Western commentators, ranging from *The Economist* to Henry Kissinger, can talk of a "Soviet-backed coup."[13] This presentation of events in South Yemen is debatable on a number of counts: first, the coup attempt was a decidedly anti-Soviet one; second, Soviet influence in South Yemen has been preponderant since the late 1960s, and it is therefore misleading to describe the 1978 events as a turning point; third, the events in South Yemen came to a head above all because of increasing pressure imposed on that country by Saudi Arabia, and not through some form of Soviet "interference"; and finally, events subsequent to June 1978 cannot be explained if it is assumed that Moscow was from then on in control of the country. Let us now consider the evidence.

South Yemen, an impoverished country of under two million people on the southwest corner of the Arabian Peninsula, has been independent since the nationalist revolution triumphed in 1967.[14] Since 1969, the leadership positions in the ruling National Liberation Front had been held by Abdul Fatah Ismail, the Secretary-General, and Salem Robea Ali, the Assistant Secretary-General and President of the country. Over the years, a number of divergences between the two emerged. These differences began with economic policy—whether to rely on the spontaneity of the masses (Salem Robea Ali), or on more orthodox centralized administrative procedure (Abdul Fatah Ismail)—and extended to what kind of party the NLF should be—a militant if loosely-structured group based on a strong ethnic element (Salem Robea Ali), or a more estab-

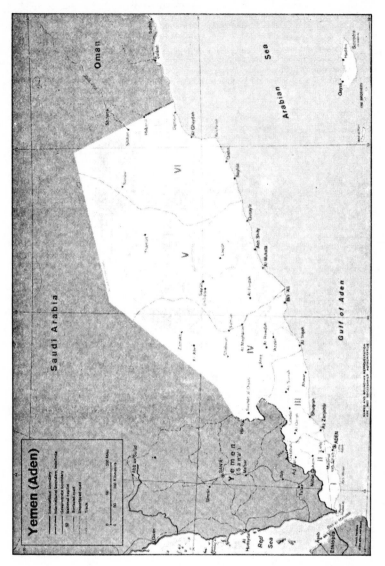

Source: U.S. Department of State.

lished formal structure modelled on the ruling parties of Eastern Europe (Abdul Fatah Ismail).

These political differences—familiar from other revolutions—were interlaced with personal, factional, and tribal **91** animosities; but they also intersected with foreign relations. Beginning in 1975, Saudi Arabia made approaches to South Yemen, trying to persuade it to break its ties with the Soviet Union, and offered aid to Salem Robea Ali in his capacity as President; Abdul Fatah, meanwhile, wanted to continue the country's close ties with the Soviet Union. This tentative opening was brought to an end by events in the Horn of Africa which provoked tension between South Yemen and the Saudis, and helped to polarize the conflict within the South Yemeni party. When the Russians were expelled from Somalia in November 1977, they were forced to bring their naval equipment (in particular a dry dock) to South Yemen, thus acquiring a direct stake in the country which they had previously lacked. Conversely the Saudis, angered by Yemeni resistance, cut off all aid and began to position troops along the frontier. And in North Yemen, along a field of conflict between forces sympathetic to either South Yemen or Saudi Arabia, the political situation also became much more acute, with the assassination of the moderate President Ibrahim al-Hamdi by Saudi agents in October 1977. By force of circumstance, South Yemen was therefore pushed much closer towards the Soviet Union, and this in turn weakened the position of the President, Salem Robea Ali.

On June 26, 1978, after months of wrangling inside the NLF over economic and international issues, Salem Robea Ali attempted a coup. But after some hours of fighting in Aden and in the town of Zinjibar, the coup failed. The President and some of his associates were executed. The debate inside the NLF and the question of South Yemen's foreign orientation was therefore settled for the time being. The Soviet Union certainly was influential in South Yemen before June 26, and benefitted from the defeat of Salem Robea Ali. But it is quite erroneous to attribute the cause of the events there to some Soviet design, and there is no evidence of a direct Russian role. As in Afghanistan, it was attempted interference by a *Western* ally, in this case Saudi Arabia, which must be the candidate for any external destabilizing role.

South Yemen conducts its politics amid considerable secrecy, and there is therefore much ground for speculation that is, of necessity, only tenuously related to hard evidence.

But the tenor of the way in which the 1978 events are presented in the West is such as to obscure the very basic and indisputable fact that South Yemen had been aligned with Moscow *since 1969,* and that this was a result of its exposed position in the predominantly conservative Arabian Peninsula. Moreover, the "Soviet coup" theory makes the conventional mistake of assuming that all internal political conflicts are the product of external interference. There was no direct Russian role in June 1978. The claim that there was produced a curious paradox when, in April 1980, the main exponent of Soviet policy, Abdul Fatah Ismail, resigned from his positions as President and Secretary-General and was replaced by then Prime Minister Ali Nasser Mohammad.

The fall of Abdul Fatah Ismail was caused by many of the same factors that undermined Salem Robea Ali in 1978: disagreements over policy toward North Yemen were growing, the concentration of political power in presidential hands was resisted by other Politburo members, and the presidential failure to manage the economy encouraged opposition. Abdul Fatah Ismail had earlier triumphed and had increased South Yemen's alignment with the U.S.S.R. —symbolized by the signing of a 20-year Treaty of Friendship—in expectation that the Soviets would respond with greater material aid. Yet such aid was not forthcoming, and as a result a definite backlash occurred. Why the Russians failed to deliver is unclear: it may have been that despite Abdul Fatah's wishes, they were not yet fully confident of the general orientation of the Yemeni leadership; and/or it may be that the economic assistance capabilities of the Soviet Union had been stretched to the limits by the demands of Afghanistan, Ethiopia, Vietnam and Cuba. Whatever the reason, the result was that by mid-1980 many of South Yemen's economic problems were being blamed upon the Russians, and especially in Aden where food shortages and cuts in electricity supply were laid at the door of the U.S.S.R. In such a situation, and with Abdul Fatah having visibly failed to obtain adequate funding from Moscow, the majority of the Politburo, including the powerful military leader Ali Antar, turned against him and voted him out of office—over the protests of the Soviet Ambassador. The fact that the Soviets had been very sympathetic to the former Minister of State Security, Mohammad Said Abdullah, who had been ousted in August 1979 and exiled to Ethiopia, was a further reason for widespread resentment. But once again it was the autonomous drive of local politics—in spite of, not at the behest of—outside powers, that shaped events in this country. In sum, the removal of Abdul Fatah Ismail was due to the failure of the Russians to capitalize on the opening which the leadership crisis of June 1978 had given them.[15]

Had the events of June 1978 constituted a "Soviet-backed coup," it is impossible to explain the events of April 1980 in which the apparently secure Soviet grip was loosened. Needless to say, the publicity accorded the "Soviet-backed coup" of 1978 by Western commentators was not accorded to the events of 1980 that disconfirmed the conventional view.

Ethiopia: The Response to Invasion

A comparable pattern of distortion can be discerned in coverage of Ethiopia.[16] From the end of the Second World War until 1974, the United States was well entrenched in Ethiopia, backing the archaic and repressive regime of Haile Selassie. Ethiopia, with a population of 33 million and a land area of 397,000 square miles (of which 65 percent can be used for agriculture), was the poorest country in Africa: in 1975, adult literacy was under ten percent, per capita income was $100, and life expectancy at birth was 38 years. Part of the responsibility for the continuation of this shameful situation must rest with the Western countries who maintained the regime and, in particular, the 40,000-strong armed forces upon which it relied to remain in power.

In February 1974 a popular movement, based on urban civilian protest and mutinies in the military, broke the power of the Emperor. He was deposed in September 1974, and replaced by a military ruling body, the Provisional Military Administrative Council (P.M.A.C.), which has been in power ever since. Was there any Soviet involvement in the events of 1974? None that has been demonstrated. There was no Communist Party, and the P.M.A.C.'s ideo-

logy was, at best, an ill-defined form of nationalistic

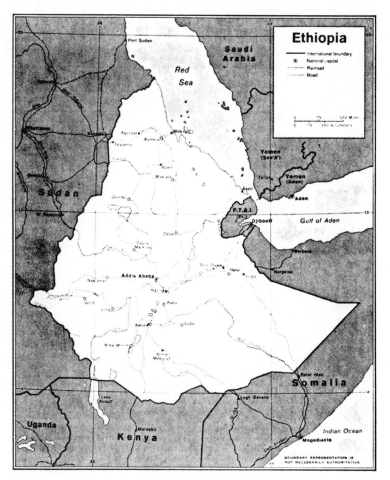

Source: U.S. Department of State.

"Ethiopian Socialism." Until early 1977, the P.M.A.C. maintained relations with the United States and, while a substantial military agreement was signed with Moscow in December 1976, this was not immediately honored by the Russians. Why then was the P.M.A.C. able to strengthen its ties with the Soviet Union in 1977 and 1978? There are four main reasons. First, in February 1977, the United States cut off all military aid to Ethiopia in protest against the internal policies of the P.M.A.C., especially with regard to human rights. Secondly, in June-July 1977, Ethiopia was invaded by neighboring Somalia at the active instigation of the conservative Arab states, particularly Saudi Arabia and Egypt, and, as will be explained below, with at least some direct encouragement from the United States. In this situation Ethiopia, cut off from its traditional source of arms, became reliant on the U.S.S.R. Thirdly, the Saudis and Egyptians were advocating a general policy of turning the Red Sea into an "Arab Lake," and, while the demand of the Eritreans for independence was a legitimate one, the Arab states were manipulating the Eritrean guerrillas and inciting the conservative Ethiopian Democratic Union (based in Somalia) in an attempt to bring down the P.M.A.C. Fourthly, the Soviet Union gave support to the radical social measures taken by P.M.A.C. inside Ethiopia—in particular the land reform measures of March 1975—and was by then convinced of the dimensions of the Ethiopian revolution.

This is not the place to go into the question of the P.M.A.C.'s internal policies with regard to human rights and the nationalities in Ethiopia: as the reports of Amnesty International show, there is much to criticize there.[17] But the fact remains that the growth of Soviet and Cuban influence in Ethiopia, culminating in the dispatch of thousands of troops and advisers in late 1977, was a reaction to events that the U.S.S.R. had not brought about. Quite simply, it was a response to the invasion of Ethiopia by Somalia. The revolution itself was caused by predominantly internal factors, as was the case in Afghanistan and Iran; the subsequent radicalization of the international situation in the Horn of Africa was a result of the policies of Washington and its allies.

It is conventionally asserted that Soviet policy in the Horn involved a "cynical" switch from the weaker state, Somalia, to the stronger one, Ethiopia. Certainly the geopolitical advantages of an alliance with a potentially strong Ethiopia cannot have escaped Soviet decision-makers. But the evidence does not bear out the force of the "cynicism" charge. First of all, the Russians waited for two and a half years before playing the Ethiopian card. A former high-ranking Ethiopian foreign office official, with access to the top government levels, told me in 1979 that the

P.M.A.C. tried, from the first day of its coming to power, to acquire substantial quantities of Soviet equipment with which to face Somalia. The Russians, he told me, refused to meet these demands for fear of antagonizing Somalia and the Arab states, including Egypt, with whom it still retained some ties. Contrary to general belief about "pro-" and "anti-" Soviet factions, this was an option universally supported within the P.M.A.C., which was aware of arms withholdings by the United States. It was the Soviet Union which would not comply. The turnaround in 1977 came not as a result of some change in mind in Moscow, but because of the change in Somalia's policy, which went on to the offensive against Ethiopia and turned against the U.S.S.R. Even here the Soviet response was controlled: the Russians first tried mediation (the Podgorny and Castro missions); then in the summer they sent in limited supplies of arms— but to northern Ethiopia, since they told the Ethiopians they could prevent a Somali attack in the southeast. The truly massive Eastern bloc intervention, involving a Soviet airlift and the deployment of several thousand Cuban troops, took place only after the Somalis had taken the further step of expelling the Russians and Cubans from their country. Somali President Siad Barre's speech announcing the expulsions came on November 13, 1977; the Soviet airlift began on November 26; the Cuban forces started arriving in December. Even then, however, the arms and troops were used exclusively to push the Somalis out of Ethiopian territory; indeed, the Russians irritated the Ethiopians by pressuring them not to engage in hot pursuit and punitive raids into Somalia. Had they wanted to do so, the Cuban-Ethiopian forces could have invaded Somalia and threatened the Somali regime itself.

Even after the Soviet and Cuban interventions in Ethiopia, the political process in that country remained far more independent of outside influence than was often believed, or than the Ethiopians and Russians themselves admitted. The majority of the Ethiopian military leadership had been trained in the United States and, despite their espousal of a new revolutionary politics, were critical of the U.S.S.R. Ethiopia differed with Moscow on a wide range of issues: on Eritrea where, despite the reprehensible Soviet assistance to the Ethiopians, there were considerable divergences (with the Russians favoring a negotiated rather than a military settlement); on the question of party-building, with both the Russians and Cubans trying to influence the formation of a new party and annoying the Ethiopians by bringing back into the country a leader of the Left-wing Me'ison Party, Negede Gobezzie, who had fled Mengistu's regime; on Zimbabwe, where the Ethiopians favored Mugabe as against the Soviet-backed Nkomo; and on economic matters, where the Ethiopians delayed in working out repayment terms for the Soviet arms, resisted Soviet pressures to buy Ilyushins for Ethiopian Airlines, and expressed open dissatisfaction with the quality of Eastern bloc equipment, particularly East German trac-tors.[18] The P.M.A.C. itself reportedly contained a group of officers considered more sympathetic to the Soviet Union, but they remained in a less influential position than the more nationalist forces loyal to Chairman Mengistu. As in South Yemen, it appears that despite a general alliance with the Soviet Union, Ethiopia's internal politics and policies remain largely beyond Soviet control. Indeed, the level of nationalist sentiment in Ethiopia is such that the Russians are likely to find their position there signifi-cantly reduced in the future, once the external threats facing the Ethiopians—in Eritrea and along the border with Somalia—are felt to have been overcome.[19]

These four summaries point to one fundamental con-clusion: political change in these four "crisis" countries was not controlled, dominated or even significantly manipu-lated by the Soviet Union. To use Kissinger's idiom, it was not Moscow which set the rockslide in motion. There were, however, important consequences for the Soviet Union and advantages did arise, some of which were taken. This discussion forms the subject matter of Chapter VII. Before assessing the implications for Soviet policy, how-ever, it is relevant to examine the crucial role which the West, despite appearances, played in these crises. It is this dimension which forms the topic of Chapter VI.

VI:
THE UNITED STATES AND ITS ALLIES: THE FALLACY OF INACTION

Since the prevailing view of events in the four "crisis countries" is one that ascribes a leading role to *Soviet* policies, it may be easier to set this Soviet role in its proper perspective if other significant causal factors are re-introduced into the analysis. The U.S.S.R. has certainly played an active role in the conflicts that have overtaken these four countries since the mid-1970s. The dispatch of troops to Afghanistan and of military supplies to Ethiopia, to take the two most outstanding cases, are significant international initiatives, by any standards. But this does not prove that the U.S.S.R. is guilty of the New Cold War charges, nor that it was the only power to influence the course of events. Any full account of what happened in the Arc would have to give proper weight to the U.S. role in these events. To be sure, much of what is claimed by the Russians, or by the Iranians and Ethiopians, about the U.S. role, is baseless or greatly exaggerated. It forms part of the persistent Left-wing and Third World exaggeration of the role of the United States, the effect of which is to shift responsibility for all internal problems onto the actions of external powers. But conversely, the assumption of U.S. uninvolvement that underlies much Western discussion is also rather wide of the mark. One can, indeed, identify three types of U.S. contributions to the crises of the Arc, contributions that are conventionally overlooked in the New Cold War presentation of regional events. The first is a historical contribution: the impact of postwar U.S. policy on these countries. The second concerns the role which U.S. policy, and that of its regional allies, had in sparking off the crisis in question. The third concerns actions taken by the United States and its allies in influencing the course of events after the crises had begun.

The Roots of Revolution: Washington's Contribution

In two of the four Arc countries, Iran and Ethiopia, the impetus for a mass revolution, and the depth of hatred ultimately unleashed, correlated with substantial U.S. support over a quarter of a century for the imperial despots who ruled these states. American support for Haile Selassie was based on the desire to retain the U.S. communications base at Kagnew, near the Eritrean capital of Asmara, and to preserve an influential pro-Western regime in power. Although some suggestions for reform were made by the U.S. Embassy in the 1960s, these came to nothing and were not repeated. U.S. military aid to Ethiopia, totalling $279 million from 1951 to 1976, was almost half of all such aid to Black African states. Much of the $350 million in economic aid was pocketed by Ethiopian officials. One U.S. Ambassador to Ethiopia summed up the official U.S. attitude to military aid as follows: "It was really Kagnew rent money, and if the Emperor wanted it in 'solid gold Cadillacs,' he could have it that way."[1] Meanwhile, the Ethiopian population lived in conditions of repression and neglect. And when the regional revolts in Eritrea and Bale threatened the regime in the 1960s, U.S. arms and advisers were used in the counterinsurgency efforts.

In Iran, U.S. military aid dates back to 1942. In 1946, U.S. advisers helped crush socialist movements in Azerbaijan and Kurdistan. Seven years later, in the now famous coup of August 1953—when the Shah deposed the legally elected government of Dr. Mosadeq—C.I.A. advisors played an active role beside the U.S.-trained army.[2] From then on, right through the 1960s and 1970s, U.S. advice and support was essential to the Shah's regime. Not only did this aid involve the conventional arms provided the Iranian army, but it also went right to the heart of SAVAK, the secret police: SAVAK was set up in 1957 with the help of C.I.A. and F.B.I. advisers, and many of its officials were trained at the Marine Corps training center at Quantico, Virginia. A former chief analyst with the C.I.A. in Iran has now revealed that the C.I.A. trained SAVAK officials in interrogation techniques.[3] Given the close relations between the two intelligence services there is no way the C.I.A. could have been ignorant of SAVAK's widespread use of torture against opponents of the regime.

Yet U.S. officials consistently denied that evidence for torture was conclusive, and we find Alfred Atherton, later Ambassador to Cairo and U.S. representative at the Shah's funeral, telling Congress that torture no longer took place. If one adds to this the enormous deliveries of weapons to the Shah, making Iran the world's top customer for U.S. arms in the mid-1970s, it becomes easier to determine which external power most contributed to a situation in which a popular revolution occurred in Iran.

Regional Destabilization: The Nixon Doctrine and Beyond

Many of the alleged Soviet "advances" in the Arc have been made possible by the acts of the United States or of its regional allies, whose capacity depends crucially on Western support. The Nixon Doctrine, propounded in July 1969, allocated a militant new counter-revolutionary role to key Third World states, among them Saudi Arabia and Iran. The Carter-Brzezinski policy of backing what are called "regional influentials" followed the same path.

In Afghanistan, as we have seen, the key factor that led to Daud's downfall was his growing alliance with Iran. The Shah felt Afghanistan to be a country that Iran could dominate: it was ruled by Iran in the eighteenth century, a third of its population speak Persian, and it could provide some of the raw materials Iran needed for industrialization. The Shah's plan for an Asian Common Market, deliberately seen as a bloc of Aryan (i.e., non-Arab) countries including Pakistan, Afghanistan, and India, was really an attempt: (a) to dominate Southwestern Asia strategically or, as with India, to form a dominant coalition; and (b) to acquire the raw materials and labor Iran needed for its economic growth. The attempt to subjugate Afghanistan led in the end to a revolt that was in the first place political but had strong nationalist and potentially social consequences. Even further back, however, the role of U.S. policy in laying the groundwork for these events can be discerned. For Afghanistan, ruled by a backward monarchy, only turned to the Soviet Union for arms in the mid-1950s after the United States refused to supply it. The reason for this refusal was U.S. support for Pakistan, Afghanistan's regional competitor. It was American hostility in this regard, including the forced incorporation of Pakistan into the SEATO and CENTO military alliances, which pushed the archaic ruling class of Afghanistan into a military dependence on the U.S.S.R. While the Russian advisers evidently did not exploit their presence in the Afghan Army to organize the 1978 coup, the growth of Leftist sentiment owed a great deal to the fact that from the mid-1950s onwards, thousands of Afghans—military and civilian—received training in the U.S.S.R.

A similar set of developments can be discerned in the Horn of Africa. As we have seen, the record shows that the Soviet-Cuban policy of supporting the Ethiopians developed by stages, each stage being *preceded* by an escalation from the Somalis and the West. The Somalis, on the basis of understandings given them, believed that the West would come to their aid and would support them in an attempt to hold onto part of Ethiopia after their invasion in 1977. This was a mistaken belief, and the U.S. government has always denied that it encouraged any such Somali belief. Yet the record, if carefully examined, shows a rather less convincing picture. Efforts to woo Somalia away from the Soviet Union go back to the early 1970s, when Saudi Arabia—alarmed at the Russian presence in the Somali port of Berbera—offered the Somalis a substantial amount of money in return for the expulsion of the Russians. The Somalis were interested, and even offered the United States basing facilities at the port of Kismayu. Yet even though backed by U.S. officials in Saudi Arabia, the deal was vetoed by Kissinger. His reasoning was that the Soviet position in Somalia constituted a useful legitimization for expansion of the much more substantial and, as it turned out, permanent U.S. naval facility on the island of Diego Garcia.[4] However, when Jimmy Carter came to office in January 1977, new overtures were made to Somalia. In April, he was ostentatiously reported by *Time* magazine as telling the State Department that "I want them to move in every possible way to get Somalia to be our friend." On June 11, 1977, he made a major speech outlining plans to 102 "aggressively" challenge the Soviet Union for influence in a number of countries, among which he named Somalia. And on July 15, 1977, the State Department officially announced its willingness, in principle, to supply Somalia with "defensive weapons."

This new U.S. offering did not amount to a commitment to support the occupation of the Ogaden, but the Somalis also claim that they received private encouragement on this score from the U.S. government, via a personal envoy, Dr. Kevin Cahill. Cahill is an expert on tropical medicine, a medical consultant to Somali President Siad Barre and a force in Democratic Party politics in New York. He visited Somalia in the early summer of 1977 and met with Siad Barre. According to the Somalis he told them: (a) that the U.S. would not resupply Ethiopia with arms in the event of a Somalia attack upon the Ogaden; and (b) that the U.S. would not "look askance" at such an attack. While the State Department at first denied that Cahill had had any such mission, it later emerged that he had indeed had a briefing discussion with the Legal Counsellor at the Department, Matthew Nimetz. And neither Nimetz nor Cahill have clarified what they in fact discussed, a reticence that can only reinforce suspicions.[5]

As events transpired, guerrilla actions backed by Somalia had started in June 1977, and the Somalis sent their regular army into the Ogaden within two weeks of the U.S. arms sales announcement of July 15. In early August the U.S. went back on its commitment to supply arms; while some members of the Administration *had* favored such a policy, the government as a whole was not prepared openly to support the Somali move, and Kenya had put strong pressure on Washington not to arm the Somalis (who still claimed part of northern Kenya as well). But the C.I.A. did send some covert supplies to the Somalis,[6] and there is enough evidence to show that it was the signals from Washington to Siad Barre, combined with material support from the Arab world, which led the Somalis to take the decision to go into Ogaden. However much Washington has tried later to absolve itself from responsibility in this matter, it played a substantial, even if not decisive, part in detonating the crisis. Given their nationalist claim, the Somalis did not need any Arab or American aid to contemplate an invasion, but it was this sense of outside support **103** which, on top of the weakness of the Ethiopian government, led to the invasion decision.

Once the Somali invasion began, the rest of the scenario followed: the Russians increased their commitment to Ethiopia, the Somalis then expelled them, the Cubans came into Ogaden. In 1980, the United States again agreed to sell arms to Somalia and started negotiations for acquisition of its own military bases in that country. Yet it is continued Arab and now Western backing for Somalia that, by reinforcing Somali militancy, ensures that the Cubans will stay in Ogaden longer than would otherwise be the case. On their side, the Cubans have stated that they have troops in Ethiopia, as they have them in Angola, to protect a legitimate government against external attack, and that they will leave Ethiopia when Somali aggression ceases. The Cubans deny that their role involves them in Ethiopia's internal affairs—a position that theoretically precludes them from any involvement in Eritrea. The Eritreans would, of course, deny that their struggle forms an "internal" affair of Ethiopia's, since they claim their territory is a separate country. But the distinction made by the Cubans nevertheless serves to explain why their forces are in Ethiopia, and underscores the Somali responsibility for this continued state of affairs.[7]

South Yemen is another case of Western and Saudi involvement. Since Yemen's independence in 1967, the Saudis have—with Western encouragement—repeatedly harassed the South Yemeni government and have involved the Aden regime in further conflicts by intervening to sustain rightist regimes in South Yemen's two smaller neighbors, North Yemen and Oman. The Saudis fought a brief war with South Yemen in 1969, and they later armed tribesmen who were sent into the South to carry out sabotage missions. They also imposed an aid blockade on the South Yemenis, refused to recognize it until 1975, and even refused to sell oil to South Yemen at below world prices after 1973, despite their normal rhetoric about "Arab brotherhood." Faced with such a regional threat, and with a denial of Western aid and a Saudi refusal to recognize it until nine years after independence, South Yemen had to rely increasingly on the Soviet Union for military assistance, and it was only in 1980 that a semblance of normal relations between these two Arabia Peninsula countries was established.

The lesson of all three countries—Afghanistan, Ethiopia, South Yemen—is therefore the same: that the development of the internal crises was in part precipitated by the policies of the West and its allies.

The U.S. Response: Self-Fulfilling Prophecies

The U.S. reaction to developments in the Arc has often been such as to exacerbate the situation at hand. In some cases, one can argue that the response of Washington, and of its regional allies, virtually *forced* the governments involved to turn to Moscow for assistance. The case of Somali-Ethiopia conflict in the Ogaden needs little further elaboration, and the U.S. decision in early 1980 to seek basing rights in Somalia clearly ran the risk of prolonging the Soviet-Cuban presence in Ethiopia. As already explained, the Cubans are primarily there to protect the Ethiopian frontier with Somalia, and it is this frontier which, by making new deals with Somalia, the United States reinflamed. The Somalis have now given Washington assurances that they will not send regular forces to Ogaden. But they gave similar assurances to the Russians in the early 1970s, and there is no reason to suppose that if they had an opportunity they would not do so again. The presence of U.S. naval and air facilities at Berbera will act as a guarantee of Western support for Somalia.

In the South Yemeni case a similar self-fulfilling antagonism has prevailed. The sale of the F-15s to Saudi Arabia in 1976, so disputed by Israel, was defended by U.S. Administration officials primarily on the grounds that there was a "threat" to Saudi Arabia from radical Arab states, specifically South Yemen and Iraq.[8] Yet much of the argumentation on which this "threat" was supposed to rest was false—e.g., the claim that South Yemen attacked Saudi Arabia in November, 1969. The most elementary comparison of the two countries' military resources and geographical relationship would have shown this "threat" to be a Pentagon fiction. In the spring of 1979, after a short border conflict between North and South Yemen, the United **105**

States tried to dispatch arms and advisers to North Yemen to counter Soviet influence—ignoring the fact that the Russians had reined in their South Yemeni allies, and that the North Yemenis were reluctant to be so visibly endowed by Washington in any case. As explained in Chapter Four, the United States fabricated a crisis for its own reasons.

The U.S. collaboration with Oman, South Yemen's neighbor on the East, has also exacerbated local conflicts: South Yemen and Oman were, during 1979, engaged in private negotiations designed to establish diplomatic relations between them. These were to end the hostility that had prevailed in previous years as a result of South Yemeni support for the rebellion against the Sultan of Oman in the southern, Dhofar, province of that country. However, the South Yemenis were not willing to establish relations if Oman granted bases to foreign countries. The British had ceased to have formal bases in Oman after several decades of tenure in 1977, and the Iranians pulled their forces out after the revolution of 1979; thus the way seemed open for some minimal reconciliation, but the U.S. decision to acquire facilities there, coupled with unconfirmed rumors of U.S. and Egyptian troop maneuvers in Dhofar itself, effectively killed off this opportunity. Instead, the Western press is replete with unsubstantiated stories about a possible South Yemeni attack on Oman, a phantasm used to justify Western arms sales and U.S. naval facilities in Oman.[9]

The U.S. also made its contribution during the Iranian revolution itself. Having armed Iran for decades, and with several thousands of U.S. military personnel in the country, the United States continued to play an active role on a day-to-day basis during the revolution. Virtually all the soul-searching about U.S. policy in Iran was about what "we" should do, and who the U.S. Embassy should work with—not about the more basic question of whether the United States should play a role at all. Washington reacted critically in November 1978 when Brezhnev warned the United States not to intervene in Iran as if no such involvement was ever contemplated; yet from the U.S. press itself we know that scores of C.I.A. experts and riot-control specialists were flown into the country in the closing weeks of 1978.[10] Subsequently, in January 1979, the

NATO envoy General Huyser was directly involved in unsuccessful attempts to preserve the vestiges of the Pahlavi state machine. Washington's failure to influence events was a result of the collapse of the Iranian regime—not of a lack of political will in Washington.

Since the Iranian revolution, the subject of U.S.-Iranian relations has become an even more tortured one, especially after the seizure of the U.S. Embassy hostages in November 1979. Yet despite the sharpening of U.S. policy toward Iran, culminating in the embargoes and military ventures, there was no let-up in Iranian political hostility to the Soviet Union over Afghanistan. What American pressure did produce was, as we have seen, some strengthening of Iran's *economic* ties with the Soviet Union as Tehran sought to circumvent the threat of an embargo along its southern ports by expanding trading links along its northern frontier with the U.S.S.R.[11]

The most contentious of all these cases of U.S. aggravation is Afghanistan. Here the Soviet and Afghan government claims about a concerted Western policy of subversion against the P.D.P.A. government are unfounded. And by blaming the whole rebel movement on outside instigation, they occlude the fact that one of the main causes of the resistance was hostility to the policies of the central government (from April 1978 to December 1979) and then to the Soviet intervention itself (December 1979 onwards). Any computation of the reasons behind the crisis in Afghanistan would have to lay considerable responsibility on the shoulders of the P.D.P.A. leadership, as well as on those features of Afghan social structure which, irrespective of external interference, would have in any case produced an armed resistance.

Yet external interference there was, and it played an important role in arousing and sustaining the rebellion which led to the Russian intervention. Most obviously, there was the support from Pakistan which allowed its territory to be used as a base area for the guerrillas. Of this there is no doubt, given the constant reporting of it in the Western press. Nor is there much doubt that the availability of camps and refugee aid encouraged the flow of potential Afghan guerrillas to Pakistan; it is worth noting that nearly all were men—i.e., people who could and would **107** fight; the women and children, usually predominant in conventional refugee situations, stayed behind in Afghanistan. In addition, however, there was organized Pakistani military support for the rebels, with the provision of a number of camps in the border area for training in modern weapons and fighting techniques.[12] From some time early in 1979 China was also providing some military support to the rebels via Pakistan, and some Arab support—in the form of arms and weapons—was later also forthcoming.[13] U.S. arms supplies are only known to have reached the rebels in early 1980, i.e., after the Soviet intervention had begun, but the United States was encouraging its allies, Pakistan and Egypt, to provide such support prior to this date.

Subsequent to the Soviet intervention of December 1979, support for the Afghan rebels became a major plank of the Right-wing Muslim states allied to the United States —especially Egypt, Saudi Arabia, and Pakistan. In reality this aid was much less than was hoped for by the rebels or than was alleged by the Russians; but the climate of outside support helped further to inflame the rebellion inside Afghanistan itself and to contribute both to the intransigence of the Russians and their allies, and to the determination of the rebels to fight on without compromise.

Without ascribing sole responsibility to this factor, one can argue that the level of foreign support prior to the Soviet intervention in late 1979 was such that it enabled the rebellion to gather its full force, and—in an international climate marked by Soviet disillusion with the United States—it provided both the reason and the pretext for the Soviet intervention. Had Pakistan not played the base-area role it did, and had not the Chinese and Arabs provided their backing, it is much less likely that the Russians would have gone into Afghanistan directly. Since then, intervention there has been a replay of the Ogaden scenario: after sending in their own forces to stabilize a situation inflamed by hostile forces, the Russians find themselves faced with a Western response that makes any return to the *status quo ante* even more difficult. While the Russians certainly derive military advantages from being in Afghanistan, there is no evidence to suggest that the Russians want permanently to transform Afghanistan into a forward military area, on the Eastern European model, nor that they want to use it to seize the oil producing states of the Gulf. They are concerned about Afghanistan itself—about establishing a stable government there and in ensuring that hostile forces do not triumph in a country that borders their own. Given the fact that the West had no interest in Afghanistan,[14] these aims are compatible with detente and a global co-existence. Yet they are ones that the policies of the United States, and of its local allies, have made it the more difficult to attain.

There is indeed some circumstantial evidence to suggest that the confrontation over Afghanistan was welcome to both the Pakistani and U.S. governments. The Pakistanis saw a crisis with Afghanistan as a way of recouping support from the West that had been prejudiced by Pakistan's program of acquiring nuclear weapons; by fomenting trouble in Afghanistan in the expectation that it would lead to further Soviet involvement, the Pakistanis created a situation in which Washington would be more likely to disregard concern about the nuclear program and offer Islamabad substantial military assistance. This is exactly what happened: General Zia, the Pakistani President, rejected an offer of $400 million in military and economic assistance offered in early 1980; the next year the new Reagan Administration offered him military aid valued at over $2 billion. How far U.S. officials foresaw the consequences of their actions is debatable: but there is no doubt that there were those such as Zbigniew Brzezinski who saw the April 1978 coup in Kabul, and even more so the December 1979 Soviet intervention, as heaven-sent opportunities for embarrassing the Russians at very little cost to the West, which had long ago abandoned Afghanistan. British and American officials interviewed by the author in 1980 and 1981 made no secret of their view that the Afghan rebels could never win; they saw semi-covert support as a means of hitting at Russia in that country's back door. It was a replay, on a much grander scale, of the C.I.A.-SAVAK use of the Iraq Kurds' struggle in the early 1970s. The Kurds were used as part of a wider strategic game. Their backers never expected them to win. And, when it suited the Shah, he abandoned the Kurds and reached an agreement with the Iraqis.

The overall import of this chapter is therefore one which diverges from the view that Soviet agency has been the main external factor operating in the Arc of Crisis. Whatever the Russians have done, they have not been the only outsiders seeking to play a role in these countries. The analysis given here identifies a Western agency on three levels: historical involvement, promoting the crisis, and intervening to find advantage. This does not mean that the West *created* these crises: the causes lay, as we have repeatedly emphasized, in the internal processes of these states. However, those attempting to analyze external agency should look at the actions of the West as well as of the East. Once the contribution of the West has been identified, it becomes easier to evaluate that of the U.S.S.R., the supposed *primum mobile* of the Arc of Crisis. Much has already been said about the Soviet role, especially in Chapter V. The following chapter seeks to resume the general trend of Soviet actions, and to suggest an alternative critique of it.

VII:
PATTERNS OF SOVIET POLICY

Enough has been said in the two preceding chapters to indicate that the portrayal of the Russians as the main instigators of "instability" in the Arc of Crisis region is an inaccurate one. In Ethiopia and in Afghanistan, their aim has been to protect allied governments that were already in place but which were faced with substantial threats—the former by invasion from a neighboring state, the latter by a domestic rebellion armed and supported from abroad. In Iran, the Russians have not as yet played a role of any significance. In South Yemen, the Soviets have tried to sustain a government that has been ostracized by the Arab world and the West. At times, moreover, Soviet policy in the region has been one of restraining its local allies from pressing advantages that opened up for them: holding back Ethiopia against Somalia in 1978, and South against North Yemen in 1979.

Yet the Soviet Union has pursued a more assertive policy as well. It may have lost widespread influence in a number of countries; but it has, with whatever attendant problems, gained it in others. Its increases in political influence have also given it military benefits—particularly in Aden and Addis Ababa—although these in no way can be considered comparable to the position it once enjoyed in Egypt and Somalia. Moreover, as discussed in Chapter II, developments in the Arc over the latter half of the 1970s have involved changes in Soviet policy itself—towards a more active intervention on behalf of its allies. Whatever the reasons for their action, the Russians' dispatch of troops to Afghanistan marks a new phase in Soviet policy in the Third World, and has produced correspondingly negative results in the international climate.

At the same time, the Soviet Union has faced considerable difficulties in managing its policy in these countries. It no more controls the internal politics of Ethiopia than it did those of Egypt under Nasser or those of Baathi Iraq. While **111** concerned about the general trends of South Yemeni politics, it is not able to dictate or even inflect policy in that country in the way, for example, that it certainly did inflect policy in Eastern European countries in the late 1940s and 1950s. In Afghanistan, the Soviet Union was drawn deeper into the conflict by the errors of its local ally, the P.D.P.A.; into support for the April 1978 coup; into backing for the provocative policies of the Taraki and Amin regimes; and then into a full-scale military presence directed at saving the P.D.P.A. regime from extinction. However lamentable, the Afghan saga does not indicate a high level of Soviet political control there. In Iran, the Soviet Union has given verbal support to the revolutionary regime. Yet it backed the revolution belatedly, and has expressed stifled alarm both at the way the Khomeini regime has handled some of its internal policies and at the strategic implications of the protracted conflict between Iran and the United States over the hostages.

It is doubtful that the Russians have gained anything from these developments in economic terms. The U.S.S.R. is sustaining the Afghan state to the tune of several million dollars per day. It is providing considerable aid to South Yemen. It has dispatched over $1.5 billion worth of weapons to Ethiopia. In no case is there any certainty that these moves will be repaid, nor, in the cases of South Yemen and Ethiopia, is there an obvious collateral onto which the Russians could attach themselves in longer term commercial agreements. The Ethiopians continue to export their coffee to the United States. Eastern bloc support as a whole for South Yemen is also a net loss as far as donor countries go.

The one area where the Russians have gained some ground is the military. Indeed there is some reason to believe that their negative experiences with the "non-capitalist road" countries over the 1960s and 1970s have led the Russians to lay less stress on political and economic coordination with these countries and to focus on the narrower issue of military access.[1] Their naval facilities in South Yemen are far less than Western propaganda would have us believe, but the Russians are able to use Aden harbor to service their Indian Ocean ships, and to change crews.[2] In Ethiopia, the Russians have acquired an ally that could in the future play a major role in African affairs, with the largest battle-experienced black army on the continent. Afghanistan has certainly brought some military benefits: it has given the Russian army its first combat experience since World War II, enabling it to recoup somewhat the advantages of experience gained by the U.S. Army in Korea and Vietnam, and has also provided it with front lines further South than they would otherwise have had. (The advantage of the latter should not be overstated, however, since Soviet capacity to influence Iran or seize the Gulf is predominantly affected by Russia's proximity to Iran itself, and has been only marginally enhanced by the Afghan intervention, as a glance at the map will show.)

Nevertheless, the overall international balance sheet on the Afghan intervention has certainly been negative. The Soviet action there came after a substantial deterioration in East-West relations for which the United States was at least partially responsible.[3] It is probable, though it cannot be proved, that the Russians were also alarmed by what they saw as a possible growth in Chinese influence along their southern flanks. Nonetheless, the direct intervention by Russian troops in conditions of extreme political confusion—i.e., where it could not be described as a simple case of responding to external aggression—has seriously worsened the international and regional climates. It has given a strong encouragement to anti-communist sentiment in the Islamic world, at a time of growing Islamic militancy, and provided the West with the perfect issue upon which to orchestrate an international campaign against the U.S.S.R. Yet these dimensions do not appear to have been dominant in Soviet thinking: the decision to enter Afghanistan was taken, it seems, for reasons relating to the situation in that country itself. It was taken despite the international consequences, and irrespective of political or military gains and losses. Thus, if it is false to argue that the Russians entered Afghanistan because of marginal strategic benefits, it must also be false to expect them to leave in order to improve the international climate. They will only leave when the Kabul government itself is strong enough to cope with the rural opposition that remains.

Soviet policy has certainly played its part, therefore, in worsening the international climate that produced the New

Cold War. The Russians argue that the New Cold War had already begun; but this does not absolve them of all responsibility for the final outcome. Yet beyond these immediate considerations, there remains some more general aspects of Soviet policy about which doubts can be raised. These are doubts which arise not from the impact of Soviet policy on East-West relations, but from its impact on the political conditions experienced by the peoples of the region themselves.

The Soviet Union has not just given general support to the regimes it favors, but has done so in such a way as to condone or support some of their more repressive characteristics. In so doing it is reproducing in the Third World its anti-democratic character at home. The Soviet model of the Party, the monolithic structure of the press, the major role of security forces—all of these are found to a greater or lesser degree in the countries that model themselves upon or which are politically allied with the U.S.S.R. There is no evidence of Soviet responsibility for the more brutal policies of some of their allies—the "Red Terror" in Ethiopia, the mass executions of Hafizullah Amin—but the general structures of party and security forces have been shaped by Russian models and advisers.

Another negative factor in Moscow's political influence is the export of the official Soviet position on nationalities. Orthodox Soviet theory stresses that socialism guarantees freedom to the working class while in practice denying this; similarly, it guarantees the right to self-determination by ethnic minorities, including the right of secession, while in practice permitting only formal autonomy and a measure of cultural diversity.[4] This has been the pattern inside the U.S.S.R., and has been reproduced in Soviet policy towards a number of Third World countries where the nationalities issue has come up: in Nigeria, where the Russians backed the suppression of Biafra in the 1960s; in Iraq in 1972-75, where they supported the suppression of the Kurds; and, most recently, in Ethiopia, where Russian arms and advisers were used in the offensive against the Eritreans in 1978.[5] Most recent criticism has focused, and rightly so, on the Soviet role in Eritrea, where Moscow has continued Washington's policy of opposition to any secession. Yet it is often forgotten that this has its root in a much deeper pattern of Soviet policy towards the nationalities question, stretching back through Kurdistan and Biafra to Bolshevik policy toward Georgia and the Ukraine after 1917.

This record indicts not just the Soviet political system but also the Soviet model of the "non-capitalist road," where the claims about new "democratic" political institutions are rather hollow ones. In many cases, these "non-capitalist" states are merely preparing the ground for a more overt capitalism later on (e.g., the case of Egypt); in others, even where a state sector predominates in the economy and some sort of economic socialist system may be said to be possible in the future, the political institutions are devoid of any of the liberties that should and could form a part of socialist society (South Yemen). It would be mistaken to blame the tendency to political dictatorship upon the Soviet Union alone, since the indigenous political tradition and political culture of these countries are often prone to encourage such repression; but the Soviet Union's identification with these policies indicates more than the requirements of an alliance. It is consistent with providing assistance in setting up parties and state institutions that enable the indigenous anti-democratic tendencies to find a new, perhaps rather modernized, form. Soviet influence of this kind is made all the more effective in those countries where the new institutions emerged, as in the Soviet Union, from a genuine revolution. Hence they employ a democratic rhetoric that derives its legitimacy from its revolutionary origins.

Far from being single-mindedly inimical to the West, Soviet policy has, too often, allowed itself to be swayed from pursuing local advantages by tactical considerations arising from concerns over the thrust of East-West relations. Such initiatives have run *counter* to the popular movements in the region. In some cases, this involves playing too cautious a role precisely in order not to antagonize the West. Soviet indulgence to the Shah and its delay in openly backing the Iranian revolution is a striking case of this, as is the earlier failure of the Tudeh Party in Iran to oppose the American-supported coup of 1953. It would have done far more for the emancipation of the people of Iran and for the prestige of the Soviet Union if it had adopted a more, not **115** less, intransigent position on these occasions. At other times, the Soviet desire to rival the West leads it into courting some of the more repressive Right-wing leaders of the Third World who may have a disagreement of greater or shorter duration with their Western allies. Notorious cases of this outside the region include support for Idi Amin of Uganda, Macias Nguema Biyago of Equatorial Guinea, and Jorge Videla of Argentina. In the Middle East, Soviet collusion with the Shah of Iran, including the sale of arms, was another case of such an alliance. Moscow's tolerant silence on Khomeini—whose hostility to socialism and whose repression of the Left are beyond doubt—is yet another case.

The failure to adopt an uncompromisingly critical stand on the issue of the U.S. hostages in Iran also followed the line of indulgence. Perhaps, as one Soviet official tried to persuade me, this was not just to humor Khomeini but also a reflection of the depth of Russian anger at Washington over the general deterioration in East-West relations. In any case, by coalescing with a general indulgence towards an anti-American Iran, it also led the Soviet authorities to be silent about the growing levels of repression inside Iran that accompanied the crisis over the hostages. One can also assume that Moscow encouraged the Tudeh Party in its policy of supporting the Right-wing clerical forces of the Islamic Republican Party against President Bani-Sadr and the Left opposition.

No survey of Soviet policy would, however, be complete without recognition of the attempts Moscow has made to meet the United States in a compromising spirit. The image of the Soviet Union as unequivocally challenging the United States throughout this region is not sustainable. Indeed there is a recurrent pattern of Soviet attempts to manage its relations with the United States in order to avoid confrontation over local conflicts, and of U.S. rejection of such negotiation offers. In the mid-1950s, for example, the Russians proposed that neither superpower sell arms to the Middle East. The U.S. refused, as this was seen as a Soviet ploy to redress an imbalance of influence in its disfavor at a time when the United States was a far larger provider of military equipment.[6] From the late 1960s

onwards, the Russians have offered to negotiate a ban on

non-indigenous bases and warships in the Indian Ocean in line with proposals made by a number of littoral states, particularly India. Again, this has been portrayed as a Soviet attempt to remove the United States from an area where the West retains an advantage. When the Russians did manage to join the Americans in a unified position, on the Arab-Israeli question in October 1977, this initiative was soon rendered null by the unilateral U.S. moves, leading to Sadat's separate peace with Israel.

As we have seen, similar Soviet attempts at compromise can also be detected in the individual components of the Arc of Crisis. In the Horn, the Russians tried to reconcile the Somalis and Ethiopians, and their efforts were undone partly by Arab and U.S. encouragement of the Somalis. Later it was Soviet restraint upon the Ethiopians, coupled with a U.S. refusal to back the Somali intervention in Ogaden, which limited the repercussions of that war in early 1978. In South Yemen, the Russians held back their local allies in the border war of February 1979. There are strong indications that they have encouraged the South Yemenis both to resolve their differences with Saudi Arabia and to improve relations with Oman. In Iran, the Russians have urged, and practiced, non-interference on the part of great powers. In Afghanistan they certainly intervened, but this was to assist an established regime that had been threatened by a rebellion in which foreign interference played a role. Yet the Russians claim their presence is not intended to be permanent, and that they will withdraw once outside interference ceases—and this means once Pakistan ceases to allow its territory to be used for armed operations and the transit of military supplies. They, and the Kabul government, are quite willing to negotiate with Pakistan on disputed issues.[7]

The most significant and neglected of all such Soviet initiatives concerns the Persian Gulf, where the pattern of Western dismissal is once again repeating itself. Far from seeking to deprive the West of its oil, the evidence suggests that the Russians realize the West's need for Gulf oil and are trying to make their acceptance of this clear. Thus, in February 1980, they called for an international conference to discuss the security of oil supply routes and the commercial access of all countries to the Gulf.[8] Brezhnev reopened **117** this offer in a keynote speech to the Indian Parliament in December 1980, and in his speech to the Twenty-Sixth Congress of the C.P.S.U. in February 1981. Yet this offer was not taken up by the West, and the conventional Western picture remains one of the Russians trying to squeeze the West out of the region. The reasons for the Western refusal to go deeper, however, than mere suspicion of Soviet intentions: as with the Soviet offers of the 1950s, the West has, at the moment, a predominant strategic position in the Gulf which it is not willing to see subjected to any negotiation. The Western countries are also resistant to the idea that the Russians should have any commercial access to oil supplies at all. As so often in the Arc of Crisis, the West's alarmism turns out, on closer examination, to be at least as much a product of its own purposes as of the visible actions or probable intentions of the Soviet leadership.

CONCLUSION:
WHAT KIND OF "RULES" FOR THE ARC?

We began this study by outlining the development of the view of a Soviet threat to the Arc of Crisis, and the reasons this region has acquired such importance in recent years. By examining Soviet relations with the region, and by reconstructing the crises of four particular countries, an attempt has been made to provide an alternative view of Soviet actions. It is now possible to summarize the main strategic conclusions of this study and to outline alternatives for Western policy based on these conclusions.

I. While much of the current Western analysis of Soviet policy in the Middle East is unfounded, there is no doubt that the U.S.S.R. *has* a policy there. This is related both to its specific internal needs (economic and political) and to its search for global parity with the United States. It supports political forces sympathetic to it, provided this is not at the expense of viable global concerns, and hopes to be able to use its military aid *both* for increased influence and for supply facilities. If the Arab world suddenly became communist of its own volition, the Russians would not actively dissuade it. But, as their policy towards communist parties in Western Europe shows, they would exert themselves to ensure that this did not so threaten Western economic interests that it led to retaliatory action.

II. There is much loose talk in Western strategic discussions of a possible direct Russian intervention in the region—crossing frontiers, sending in troops, and blocking Western oil supplies. The Russians presumably have the capacity to undertake such operations; but—a point often obscured—they could do so only in the event of a World War. They are, on their side, equally conscious of their own vulnerability to the south: of the West's capacity to block the exist from the Black Sea, to attack the U.S.S.R. from bases in the Middle East and to launch missiles from submarines in the Indian Ocean. The likelihood of Middle **119**

Eastern theater operations during a Third World War should not be confused with whether or not such a wider war is likely to start as a result of a specific Soviet offensive in this area. The intervention in Afghanistan is, as we have seen, an exceptional case, taking place in a country where the Russians had already been strategically dominant for two decades and where a pro-Soviet government was already in power.

III. The history of Russian relations with the Arab world has been a vivid reminder of the inadequacies of using the term "superpower" to describe the Soviet Union. First of all, this term implies a political equivalence between the United States and the U.S.S.R., an assumption that they operate internally and internationally in broadly similar ways. Certain similarities definitely pertain, but the differences in their method of operation are far more striking. Indeed the basis of their rivalry is the asymmetry of the two social systems, which is precisely why no permanent and comprehensive accommodation is possible. Secondly, by focusing on one undeniable aspect of the "super" relationship—the power of super-destruction—this term obscures the limits that both powers encounter in dealing with countries that are, at first sight, rather dependent on them. The Soviet inability to influence events in Egypt, or Iraq, despite these governments' reliance on Soviet military support, indicates the limits of their power (as does, in a different way, their lack of major influence on the internal affairs of another major Third World aid recipient, India). Not only have they been unable to consolidate a stable relationship with the Arab states, apart from South Yemen, but they now face the humiliation of being evicted from the rejectionist camp by the Peninsular oil producers. Given the prevalence in the Middle East of exaggerated beliefs in the influence of outside powers, it is essential to keep the *limits* of their influence in view to see the ways in which they are less than "super."

IV. There has been an overall shift in Soviet foreign policy in the past two decades, partly because the U.S.S.R. now possesses an increased military capacity, and partly because of changes in the region. This has enabled it to assist revolutionary governments where this might previously not have been possible (China, Vietnam, Angola,

Afghanistan, South Yemen). Nevertheless, this capacity has had almost no impact on the Arab Middle East, and has coincided with the shift to the peripheral states. Soviet advances are either marginal (South Yemen) or more precarious than they at first sight appear (Afghanistan, Ethiopia). The change in international relations has coincided with the rise of anti-communist oil producers as regional influences in the Middle East, and with the Khomeini-inspired wave of Islamic radicalism. The Russians seem to believe that sooner or later the U.S.-backed initiatives on the Arab-Israeli question are bound to fail and that when they do, their moment may come again. But the record of the past quarter century must give them little comfort and they are likely in the future to encounter many of the same problems that they did before.

V. An alternative critique can be made in terms, not of how Soviet policy has affected the West, but of how it has affected the peoples of the Middle East and the cause of their emancipation. Here there is always a danger of Leftist abstraction—of criticizing the Soviet Union for not doing things which it was incapable of doing, or which would have led to very serious international consequences. Moreover, some cases of Soviet restraint are ones which can well be justified: their critique of the more chauvinistic Arab utterances vis-a-vis Israel is a valid one. So too is their attempt to criticize the classless concepts of Arab unity which Middle Eastern leaders have propounded. Yet, within the realm of possibility and making allowances for what may be adventurist criticisms of Soviet policy, their record is open to substantial criticism: despite the considerable assistance which they have given in the economic and military fields, their aid in economic development has been deficient in quality and quantity. As in the rest of the world, they have subordinated local communist groups to their own policies, and thereby forced them to follow the zigzags of Moscow policy. Nowhere is this clearer than in Iran, where the Left is still paying the price of the communist errors of the 1940s and 1950s, or in Egypt, where the Left was forced to dissolve itself into the ruling party. The Russian political impact has also involved the reproduction of bureaucratic models of political organization; were Arab communists to come to power, it is probable that they would **121** reproduce societies as undemocratic as that in the U.S.S.R. itself. Even the question of Soviet Jewry throws into question the negative impact of Russian domestic policy, since the real issue at stake is not that of emigration but the failure of the Russian leadership to stamp out anti-semitism at home. The conclusion which all this suggests is that the Soviet Union has done too little, rather than too much, to assist the liberation of the Middle East; the rulers of the region, and their Western supporters, have faced less of a challenge than, given different political conditions in Moscow, they might have had to confront.

VI. Despite the level of Soviet economic ties with the region, there are no adequate grounds for embracing the most militant Left critique and seeing Soviet policy as "imperialist"—unless this term is used in a very generic way to denote the influence of a major power with international interests. If the term is used because of strictly economic factors, then the U.S.S.R. has probably not gained substantially from its ties to the Middle East, bearing in mind the loss of $7 billion loaned to Egypt. They bargain over the terms for their exports and imports, but this, on its own, does not constitute imperialism. Their aid programs to Ethiopia, South Yemen, and Afghanistan, certainly constitute deficits for the U.S.S.R. Western prognoses of a major Soviet dependence on oil in the 1980s would, if true, alter the material dependence of the U.S.S.R. on the region; but, as we have seen, this reliance is not as certain as its proponents claim. If the Soviet Union is seen as "imperialist" for political reasons, because it has supported governments that at times oppress the Left, then this would have to apply to the Russia of the early 1920s too, and, even more so, to Mao's China—something proponents of this "theory" are generally reluctant to admit.

VII. As discussed in Part I, the prime concern of the Soviet Union remains the security of its own frontiers and the avoidance of war with the United States. Clearly there are areas of rivalry with the West. The U.S.S.R. represents an alternative social system and, insofar as it supports those sympathetic to its goals, it can be said to have a "grand plan." But in this sense, the West also has such a "plan." And the recent history of Soviet policy does not indicate that it is intending to, or capable of, subjecting the

Middle East to its domination. Recent changes in the Southwest Asia/Northeast Africa region cannot be laid at the door of Soviet policy initiatives, nor have Soviet responses been any more "inconsistent" with detente than those of the West have been. Overall, recent developments in the Arc do not conform to a simple picture; a recognition of this complexity tells us more about Soviet policy and about the countries than the variants of a demonic image that have become orthodoxy in Western strategic discussions.

It is now possible to return to the theme with which this study began: the claim by Western commentators and politicians that Soviet policy in the Arc of Crisis has constituted a violation of detente, and is a prime cause, even *the* prime cause, of what can be termed the New Cold War. It should be apparent that examination of the evidence cannot sustain this charge, let alone the belief held by Mr. Reagan that Moscow is primarily responsible for the upheavals in the area. To show this is not, however, sufficient: some alternative lines of policy emerge from this analysis and will be summarized in these concluding remarks.

The central Western charge is that the Soviet Union has violated certain "rules" of international conduct, or of detente, by its actions in the Arc. The questions then arise of (a) what these rules are, and (b) whether the U.S.S.R. has violated them. The Russians would naturally add question (c), whether the United States has violated them. So far as the public record goes, there is no formal negotiated agreement on Southwest Asia comparable to other U.S.-Soviet accords, such as SALT-I, or the Helsinki agreement of 1975 on Europe. Nor could there be: great power policy in an area of sovereign states cannot be subject to the same stipulations as arms policy, or activity in a Europe which has been divided into two clear spheres since 1945. But both Soviet and American commentators suggest that there were, in the early 1970s, some mutual understandings on their policies in the Third World, which both now feel the others have broken. The Americans cite Soviet policy in Ethiopia, South Yemen and Afghanistan. The Russians cite America's policy on the Arab-Israeli dispute and the *123* build-up in the Gulf. Both would therefore seem to accept the principle of some code of conduct. Both charge the other with violations of that code.

Three problems emerge, however, from this superficial symmetry of views. First, as already indicated, no comprehensive code of conduct is possible on the European model in an area like Southwest Asia. Such an agreement presupposes a political stability and a degree of control over local states that cannot exist: indeed the local states would resist any such control were the Russians and the Americans to try to impose it. If the conception of "rules" propounded is one which denies the possibility of local interstate conflicts and of social upheavals in the Arc, then it cannot work. Secondly, the implications of the U.S. indictment of the Russians is that the latter have violated the rules by coming to the aid of their allies, or by building new alliances with states that have undergone political change: such are the charges on Ethiopia and Afghanistan. But this is a rule which Western critics would prefer not to apply to American policy: if they did, it would preclude Washington from taking advantage of Egypt's drift to the West, or of projecting its forces into the Gulf from 1979 onwards. The concept of "rules" being advanced would freeze the situation in a form most advantageous to the United States. This leads to the third and most fundamental problem: while both Americans and Russians endorse the call for "rules," their lists of "rules" coincide only partially. This is perhaps to be expected, given the asymmetrical interests of the two countries; but it has to be taken into account by both sides. No code of conduct which precludes social and political change in Third World countries will be acceptable to the Russians (Appendix One gives Brezhnev's views on this issue).[1]

Within the limits of realism and of the recognized and permanent rivalry of the two social systems, there are certain policy guidelines upon which an alternative Western approach to this area could be based. It would be one that was both more likely to find common ground with the Russians, and also would ensure that those miscalculations which have underlain Western policy in recent years do not recur:

(1) There must be a recognition of the internal causes of

social and political change in the Third World, and a rejection of the simplistic attribution of all change to Soviet manipulation. This shift in perception of what causes change should go together with some greater recognition of the degree to which Soviet advantages in some countries have, in recent years, been offset by reductions of influence in others.

(2) The United States must eschew the notion that it can re-establish control over the politics of the Arc countries. Apart from the questions of ethics, there is every reason to doubt the practicability of such a goal: the lesson of Iran is not the hard-line revisionist view that more should have been done, but rather that an exaggerated view of the United States' ability to control the policies of a Third World state will inevitably generate trouble in the future. Moreover, the call for a return to the strategies of the early 1950s rests upon a basic failure to recognize how radically economic and political conditions in the Middle East have been permanently altered.

(3) There must be some recognition of how Western policies have contributed to upheavals in the Third World, and of how current Western policies in other areas, such as southern Africa, may be laying the groundwork for new strategic crises in the future. The note of innocence struck on Angola, Afghanistan or Ethiopia is simply not sustainable: nor will it be when the inevitable explosions in South Africa occur. If there is an almost universal tendency on the part of Soviet and Third World commentators to overstate the degree of U.S. responsibility for events in the Arc and similar regions, there is a converse tendency for U.S. commentators to understate or overlook this factor.

(4) There has to be a reduced and more sober approach to what "rules" are possible and which ones are impossible. Any accusations of "rule-breaking" by one side against the other have to be matched by a willingness of those invoking that rule to respect it themselves. At times a note of rather shrill rivalry comes into the discussion on "rules" without much consideration of how consistent such charges may be, or how practical the "rules" so involved may be.

(5) Once a degree of realism and balance has been introduced, it is possible to work within such a framework for substantive mutual agreements on a wide range of **125**

issues. The Russians and Americans have found common ground on other fronts, and there is no reason why, within the limits outlined, such common ground could not be found in the Arc itself. This involves a willingness to negotiate on issues in dispute and a greater degree of collaboration in tackling the problems of the region: the Gulf, the Arab-Israeli dispute, the Horn of Africa and Afghanistan are all areas where such negotiation is possible. Initiatives in these areas would be possible in combination with local states that maintain good relations with both major powers. Kenya has close ties to the West, but also enjoys good relations with Ethiopia and could assist in negotiations on the Horn. India favors negotiation on Afghanistan, as do a number of Western European countries. India also favors demilitarization of the Gulf and of the Indian Ocean. Quite a number of Arab states favor involving the Soviet Union in negotiations on the Arab-Israeli question, among them such pro-Western states as Kuwait and Jordan.

The lesson of this study can therefore be summarized as follows: the events of the Arc of Crisis cannot be reduced to a simple picture of Soviet trouble-making, and Soviet policy is one that permits substantial negotiation between East and West on issues of concern in the region. A straightforward adversary policy both is not justified by the facts, and fails to realize the potential for reducing tension that exists. If this is a picture of the Arc more complex than that offered by the "Soviet threat" proposition, it does, I would argue, bear some closer resemblance to the truth. And it should, in the longer run, be a better guide to preserving the peace of the world and guaranteeing the interests of the peoples of the region itself.

FOOTNOTES

Preface

1. "Arc of Revolutions," *Race and Class*, (Spring, 1979); *Arabia without Sultans* (New York, 1975); *Iran: Dictatorship and Development* (New York: Penguin, 1979); "Yemen's Unfinished Revolution: Socialism in the South," *MERIP Reports* 81 (October, 1979); "Revolution in Afghanistan," *New Left Review* 112 (November-December, 1978): "War and Revolution in Afghanistan," *New Left Review* 119 (January-February, 1980); co-authored with Maxine Molyneux, *Revolution in Ethiopia* (London, 1981).

Chapter I

1. Quoted in *New York* magazine, March 9, 1981.
2. *The New York Times*, February 1, 1980.
3. Robert Tucker, *Commentary*, November 1980.
4. See Fred Kaplan, *Dubious Specter: A Skeptical Look at the Soviet Nuclear Threat* (Washington, D.C.: Institute for Policy Studies, 1980); Kaplan, "NATO and the Soviet Scare," *Inquiry* (June 12, 1978), pp. 16-20; Rep. Les Aspin, "What Are the Russians Up to?", *International Security* (Summer 1978), pp. 30-52; Aspin, "Judge Not by Numbers Alone," *Bulletin of the Atomic Scientists* (June, 1980), pp. 28-33; Arthur Macy Cox, "The Truth About Soviet Arms Spending," *New York Review of Books*, November 6, 1980, pp. 21-24; George F. Kennan, "The Soviet Threat: How Real?" *Inquiry* (March 17, 1980), pp. 15-18; and Franklyn D. Holzman, "Dollars or Rubles: The C.I.A.'s Military Estimates," *Bulletin of the Atomic Scientists* (June, 1980), pp. 23-27.
5. *World Bank Atlas* (Washington, D.C.: World Bank, 1981), p. 28. For a lucid account of the weakening of the U.S. economic position vis-a-vis its allies see Lester Thurow, "The Moral Equivalent of Defeat," *Foreign Policy* 42 (Spring, 1981).
6. For a survey of new strategies of U.S. intervention in the Gulf, and the preparations for such action, see Michael T. Klare, *Beyond the Vietnam Syndrome* (Washington, D.C.: Institute for Policy Studies, 1981), Chapter 3.
7. See the introduction to the U.S. edition of *Arabia Without Sultans* for discussion of the 1974 U.S. invasion threats. The International Energy Agency was established in 1976 to coordinate Western policy in the face of OPEC.
8. Michael T. Klare, *War Without End* (New York: Knopf, 1972), Chapter 11, foresaw a "Great South Asian War," with the center of gravity shifting from Indochina westwards.
9. *Time*, January 15, 1979.
10. *Ibid.*, January 15, 1979.
11. *Ibid.*, January 15, 1979. Others were less solemn in their geopolitical speculations: the *International Herald Tribune* conjured up a "Rhomboid of Rhetoric," while Alexander Cockburn in the *Village Voice* discussed a "Pretzel of Provocation."

12. The first Cuban unit of 700 men arrived in Angola in October 1975, fifteen months after the C.I.A. operation there began. Soviet arms had ceased being supplied to the MPLA guerrillas in 1973, and only restarted in March 1975 (John Stockwell, *In Search of Enemies* (New York: Norton, 1978)).

13. Kissinger's views are given in his interview with *The Economist*, February 3, 1979, and in his SALT testimony, reproduced in *For the Record* (Boston, 1981), especially pp. 216-221, from which the above quotations are taken.

14. Tucker, *op. cit.* J.B. Kelly, *Arabia, The Gulf and the West* (New York: Basic, 1980). Kelly's dirge berates both the British and American governments for their lack of will in the Gulf—but it fails to provide a remotely convincing case of how, in the real conditions that existed, his policy could have been followed.

15. A characteristic example of this line of argument can be found in the interview given by Alexander Haig to the *Sunday Times*, February 8, 1981. Asked about Soviet and Cuban forces in Afghanistan, Ethiopia, Angola and South Yemen, Haig replies: "I hope the Soviet Union would be seeking ways of disengaging from these *illegal invasions*" (emphasis added). The only one of these four that could, by any stretch of the argument, be called "illegal" is Afghanistan: Cuban and Soviet troops were present in the other three at the express request of the governments concerned. The implication is that any Soviet or Cuban military presence in the Third World is, in Haig's view, "illegal."

16. Brzezinski in *International Herald Tribune*, December 4, 1980. The same source reports ex-Secretary of State Vance's disagreement with this: "He declared that the Soviet Union sent troops into Ethiopia to help an ally defend its territory against Somalia, that the United States warned the Russians not to invade Somalia and they did not." "We got what we wanted," Mr. Vance said.

17. *International Herald Tribune*, February 5, 1979.

18. For one account of the development of a new Congressional climate see Joshua Muravchik, *The Senate and National Security: A New Mood* (Beverly Hills, 1980).

19. On OPEC, see Kelly, *op. cit.*; on Iran, see Michael Ledeen and William Lewis, *Debacle: The American Failure in Iran* (New York: 1981). There is a cogent critique of the Ledeen-Lewis position in "Who Lost Iran?" by Shaul Bakhash, *New York Review of Books*, May 14, 1981 and, implicitly, in Barry Rubin, *Paved With Good Intentions* (New York: Oxford Univ. Press, 1980).

Chapter II

1. A nuanced account on Soviet foreign policy in the Third World is given in Eric Shaw, *Cold Peace: Soviet Power and Western Security* (London: Labour Party Publications, 1978). For more general analyses that avoid the main pitfalls of alarmist distortion, see Philip Windsor, "The Soviet Union in the International System of the 1980s," in *Prospects of Soviet Power in the 1980s*, Part II (London: International Institute for Strategic Studies, 1979): Robin Edmonds, *Soviet Foreign Policy 1962-*

1973: The Paradox of Super Power (London: Oxford Univ. Press, 1975); and Vernon Aspaturian, "Soviet Global Power and the Correlation of Forces," *Problems of Communism* (May-June, 1980). Albeit written in a polemical vein, there is a good account of the limits on Soviet policy in the Third World in Robert Legvold, "The Super Rivals: Conflict in the Third World," *Foreign Affairs* (Spring, 1979).

2. *Constitution of the Union of Soviet Socialist Republics* (Moscow, 1977), pp. 31-32.

3. See Legvold, *op. cit.*, and Aspaturian, *op. cit.* For the superiority of U.S. over Soviet Third World intervention capacities, see Barry Posen and Stephen Van Evera, "Overarming and Underwhelming," *Foreign Policy* (Fall, 1980), pp. 102-105. According to these authors, the United States spends around 25% of its military budget on Third World intervention capability, the U.S.S.R. less than 10%.

4. *The Guardian*, November 8, 1979. On Soviet economic aid to the Third World, see the C.R.S. study noted above (Chapter One, Note 4); Orah Cooper and Carol Fogarty, "Soviet Economics and Military Aid to Less Developed Countries 1954-1978," (Washington, D.C.: C.I.A., Office of Economic Research); Stephen Clarkson, *The Soviet Theory of Development* (London, 1979). Reports from Moscow at the time of the July 1980 Olympics suggested considerable resentment in the U.S.S.R. at what were seen as lavish subsidies and facilities laid on for Third World athletes.

5. Jerry Hough, *Soviet Leadership in Transition* (Washington, D.C.: Brookings Institution, 1980), p. 165.

Chapter III

1. International Institute for Strategic Studies (IISS), *Strategic Survey 1977* (London: IISS, 1978), pp. 64-68.

2. Arms Control and Disarmament Agency (ACDA) figure taken from *The Defense Monitor* (January, 1979). ACDA figures omit two Arab countries that I have included here, North and South Yemen.

3. Cooper and Fogarty, *op. cit.*, pp. 650 ff.

4. Karen Dawisha, *Soviet Foreign Policy Towards Egypt* (London: St. Martins, 1979), p. 46. Dawisha provides an excellent account of the limits of Soviet aid and the intention of the U.S.S.R. to constrain Egyptian action at this time.

5. This summary draws in particular on Helen Carrere d'Encausse's study of the nationalities and the new nationalism in the U.S.S.R., *L'Empire Eclatee* (Paris, 1978).

6. *Le Monde,* February 14, 1981.

7. Zhores Medvedev in *New Left Review* 117 (September-October, 1979), p. 27.

8. R.W. Apple in *International Herald Tribune*, November 8-9, 1980.

9. Figures on Turkmenia from *Asia Yearbook 1979* (Hong Kong: Far Eastern Economic Review). On Afghanistan from World Bank, *Afghanistan: The Journey to Economic Development* (March, 1978).

10. Of the 28,000 Soviet Jews emigrating in 1978 only 12,000 chose to live in Israel, *Le Monde,* December 28, 1979.

11. *BP Statistical Review of the World Oil Industry* (London, 1979).   **129**

12. *International Herald Tribune,* May 20, 1981.

13. *Soviet Oil and Gas to 1990* (London: Economist Intelligence Unit, December 1980). Marshall Goldman, *The Enigma of Soviet Petroleum* (London: Allen Unwine, 1980).

14. On the C.I.A.-Petro Studies contrast see *International Herald Tribune,* May 16, 1980. The original C.I.A. study was published as *Prospects for Soviet Oil Production,* ER-1977 10270 (Washington, D.C.: C.I.A., April, 1977). Further material can be found in Leslie Dienes, "The Soviet Union: An Energy Crunch Ahead?" *Problems of Communism* (September-October, 1977), and Edward Havett, "Soviet Energy: Supply versus Demand," *Problems of Communism* (January-February, 1980). Other data taken from *Le Monde,* May 29, 1979, November 15, 1979.

15. *The Guardian* (London), May 3, 1980. Peter Odell, *Oil and World Power,* Fifth Edition (London: Penguin, 1979).

16. In 1980 the U.S.S.R. began negotiations with Western European countries under which Soviet gas supplies would increase from 9 percent of their needs in 1980 to 25 percent in 1986. This caused alarm in Washington, but was hardly a sign of an energy-hungry Russia.

17. Jerry Hough, *op. cit.,* p. 131.

18. For an atypically measured evaluation of the Soviet economy see the special issue of *Time,* "Inside the U.S.S.R.," June 23, 1980; also, Alec Nove, "Problems and Prospects of the Soviet Economy," *New Left Review* 119 (January-February, 1980).

19. Schapour Ravasani, *Sowjetrepublik Gilan* (Berlin, 1973), p. 350.

20. Roy and Zhores Medvedev, *Krushchev, The Years in Power* (London, 1977), p. 175.

21. Dawisha, *op. cit.* On Yegorychev see also Alexander Dallin, *The U.S.S.R. and the Middle East,* edited by M. Confino and S. Shamir (Tel Aviv, 1973), p. 50; and Zhores Medvedev, *New Left Review* 119, p. 6.

22. Ilana Kass, *Soviet Involvement in the Middle East: Policy Formulation 1966-1973* (Boulder, CO: Westview Press, 1978), provides a detailed account of how public Soviet views diverge on the Middle East. Her analysis is partly confirmed by Mohammad Heikal, *The Sphinx and the Commisar* (London, 1978), pp. 253-254.

23. On Paputin's death see *The Observer,* February 17, 1980, and *International Herald Tribune,* March 22, 1980. Soviet officials whom I interviewed in Kabul in October 1980, denied any knowledge of this. But for an informed Russian account of the episode see Roy Medvedev, "The Afghan Crisis," *New Left Review* 121 (May-June, 1980).

24. On China's policies for the region see Yitzhak Schichor, *The Middle East in China's Foreign Policy, 1949-1977* (Cambridge, 1979), and Nigel Disney, "China and the Middle East," *MERIP Reports* 63 (December, 1977).

Chapter IV

1. There is extensive and high quality literature on Soviet policy in the Arab world. Here I have used in particular: Helene Carrere d'Encausse, *La Politique Sovietique au Moyen Orient 1955-1975* (Paris, 1975); Karen

Dawisha, *op. cit.;* Yaacov Ro'i, *The Limits to Power: Soviet Policy in the Middle East* (New York, 1979); Robert Freeman, *Soviet Policy Towards the Middle East Since 1970* (New York, 1975); Mohamed Heikal, *The Sphinx and the Commisar* (London, 1978).

2. The Soviet theory on the "non-capitalist road" is developed in Karen Brutents, *National Liberation Revolutions Today* (Moscow, 1977). It has been ably criticized by Karen Pfeifer, "State Capitalism and Development," *MERIP Reports* 78 (June, 1979); and by Joe Slovo, "A Critical Analysis of the Non-Capitalist Path," *Marxism Today* (London, June 1974). Soviet doubts on the theory are reflected in some current official discussion, see Chapter Two, Note 5.

3. There is considerable evidence to indicate that the CIA played a role in assisting the identification of communists in the 1963 repression in Iraq; see Hanna Batatu, *The Old Social Classes and the Revolutionary Movements of Iraq* (Princeton, NJ: Princeton Univ. Press, 1978), pp. 985-6. Batatu's scholarly study is the most detailed and revealing account yet available of a communist movement in the Arab world, and of the problems encountered by Arab communists in their dealings with the U.S.S.R.

4. Russian officials have confirmed this in conversation with the author.

5. A good general survey is contained in John Cooley, "The Libyan Menace," *Foreign Policy* 42 (Spring, 1981). Cooley points out that it was the Nixon Administration, not the Russians, who first allied with Qaddafi and that it was during the period of collaboration with the U.S. that Qaddafi became involved in one of his worst ventures, the massacre of the Israeli athletes at Munich in 1972.

6. "Soviet-Libyan relations have not always run smoothly. The Kremlin does not think much of the Islamic ideology propagated by the author of *The Green Book* [i.e., Qaddafi]. Moscow has until now refused to allow the Libyans to open consulates in the republics of Central Asia and has only just accepted the conversion of the Libyan Embassy in Moscow into a 'People's Bureau.' On the Middle East question itself, there have often been disagreements. Moscow and Tripoli have no basic agreement on the scope of the required Israeli withdrawal from the occupied territories, or on the convocation of an international conference, nor on the very existence of the state of Israel itself." *Le Monde,* April 26-27, 1981.

7. Information on the shift of North Yemeni policy from author's interview with North Yemeni Premier Abdel Aziz Abdul Ghani (London, November 1979); information on U.S. personnel in the Y.A.R. as of June, 1980, in *International Herald Tribune,* June 6, 1980.

8. Lt. Col. John Ruszkiewicz, "How the U.S. Lost Its Footing in the Shifting Sands of the Persian Gulf—A Case History in the Yemen Arab Republic," *Armed Forces Journal* (September, 1980), p. 72.

9. On Soviet-Palestinian relations, and on Soviet criticism of Palestinian terroristic actions, see Galia Golan, *The Soviet Union and the PLO* (London: International Institute for Strategic Studies, 1976). See also, Baruch Gurevitz, "The Soviet Union and the Palestinian Organizations," in Yaacov Ro'i, *op. cit.*

10. William Quandt, "Soviet Policy in the October Middle East War," *131*

International Affairs (London, July and October, 1977); see also Dawisha *op. cit.*, and Heikal, *op. cit.*

11. Henry Kissinger, *The White House Years* (New York: Little, 1979), p. 1279ff. See the critique by Noam Chomsky, *Inquiry* (April 7, 1980).

12. On China, see Chapter III, Note 24.

13. For Feisal, *BBC Summary of World Broadcasts,* January 1, 1974; for Khaled, *ibid.,* July 3, 1979.

14. Stephen Page, *The U.S.S.R. and Arabia* (London: International Pubn's Service, 1971), p. 81; and Dawisha, *op. cit.,* pp. 26, 33, details Khruschev's strictures on Arab nationalism.

Chapter V

1. "This talk about there being no evidence of Soviet involvement is nonsense. The KGB is there. We ought to beef up the CIA," said Richard Helms, former CIA Director and Ambassador to Iran, in *Time,* December 18, 1978. For Robert Moss, see "Who's Meddling in Iran?" *Washington Post,* November 12, 1978.

2. Iranian hostility to the U.S. was rooted in historical causes and in a rejection of the political system imposed on Iran by the coup of 1953. Yet it burst the banks of such resentment in evoking a U.S. responsibility for almost all Iran's woes, a delusion which led to the phantasmagonic conflict over the hostages. This was, as I have explained elsewhere, an "Anti-Imperialism of Fools" (*The Nation,* March 21, 1981). One key psychological aspect of the hostage crisis has not been given its due prominence: the fact that the U.S. failed to confront the Iranian revolution head-on meant that the Iranians were deprived of that victory over the U.S. which such a confrontation might have led to. The hostage crisis served as a retrospective compensation for the absence of a humiliation of the U.S. during the revolution. For an informative liberal overview of U.S.-Iranian relations, see Barry Rubin, *Paved with Good Intentions.*

3. "I think they have their people in Iran right today. I have always thought that Ghotbzadeh was probably a KGB agent; if not, he was at least Marxist," John Connally in *The New York Times,* February 21, 1980. A similar line of argument can be found in the words of Senator Percy saying that "the Carter Administration would be 'out of its mind' if it did not insist that the Russians stop 'creating chaos in other parts of the world' such as Iran," *International Herald Tribune,* February 5, 1979. What is significant about such allegations, many more of which could be adduced, is not that this came from the most influential or level-headed politicians, but that they are indicative of a general license which U.S. politicians feel they have when discussing matters of foreign affairs. On domestic matters constraints of accuracy apply; on foreign policy there are few votes to be won, or newspaper copies sold, by challenging the inaccuracies that masquerade as patriotism and vigilance.

4. The U.S. hostages confirmed on their release that the students holding them had been Rightists. One theory widely held on the Iranian Left was that the Embassy had been seized by the Peiman followers in order to head off a Left-wing seizure and preemptively to destroy docu-

ments showing that Islamic Republican Party leader Ayatollah Beheshti had been involved in discussions with U.S. officials during the last weeks of the Shah's regime.

5. "It is obvious to me that the Iranian people will reap no benefit from the stirring up of religious fanaticism and anti-communist hysteria and the endeavor to present the policy and intentions of a friendly country in a false light . . . Repression of the left end of the spectrum automatically strengthens its right end and creates favorable conditions for pressure from outside," Bovin in *Nedelya*, September 3-9, 1979, quoted in *Current Digest of the Soviet Press*, September 26, 1979. Soviet officials report that Bovin's article provoked an angry response from Foreign Minister Gromyko who castigated the journalist for his indiscretion.

6. *Pravda* of January 17, 1981, alleged that U.S. forces were preparing an invasion of Iran. It must, in all frankness, be asked just how untrue Soviet allegations were: if claims of a fullscale U.S. invasion were false, the same cannot definitely be said about all forms of U.S. action. Incoming President Reagan had indeed intimated that some military action might be taken if the hostages were not released by the time he took office.

7. I have given a more detailed analysis of the Afghan background in other articles: "Revolution in Afghanistan," *New Left Review* 112 (November-December, 1978); and "The War and Revolution in Afghanistan," *op. cit.* Other informative analyses can be found in the special issue of *MERIP Reports* 89 (July-August, 1980); on Afghanistan; "Afghanistan under the *Khald*" by Louis Dupree, *Problems of Communism* (July-August, 1979); and David Chaffetz, "Afghanistan in Turmoil," *International Affairs* (January, 1980).

8. Selig Harrison, "The Shah, Not Kremlin, Touched Off Afghan Coup," *Washington Post*, May 13, 1979.

9. Marshall Goldman, *Soviet Foreign Aid* (New York: Praeger, 1967), pp. 122-3. Goldman also writes: "The American activity that has received the most praise from the Afghans is the sale of secondhand American clothing," p. 120.

10. The Soviet account can be found in *The Truth About Afghanistan* (Moscow: Novosti Press Agency, April 1980); and in Victor Sidenko, "Two Years of the Afghan Revolution," *New Times* 17 (1980). Sidenko makes the following, significantly false, claim: "The fact that the removal of Amin took place concurrently with the beginning of the introduction of the Soviet contingent is a pure *coincidence in time,* and there is no causal relationship between the two events. The Soviet units had nothing to do with the removal of Amin and his associates. That was done by the Afghans themselves." (His emphasis.)

11. On December 26, i.e., one day after the Soviet forces began to move in and one day before he himself was overthrown, Amin gave an interview to the correspondent of the Arab newspaper *Al Sharq Al Awsat* in which he stated that he welcomed Soviet military aid in support of his regime (*Sunday Times,* January 6, 1980).

12. On how the Soviet moves went awry, see Chapter Three, Note 23.

13. For Kissinger and *Economist* allegations, see Note 1 above; similar claims have been made in more academic literature, as for example by Donald Zagoria, "Into the Breach: New Soviet Alliances in the Third

World," *Foreign Affairs* (Spring, 1979), who cites the June 1978 events in South Yemen as part of the record of "irresponsible Soviet conduct in the Third World."

14. A detailed account of the background to events in both North and South Yemen is given by David Hirst in *The Guardian,* August 29-31, 1978. See also my "Yemen's Unfinished Revolution: Socialism in the South," *MERIP Reports* 81 (October, 1979).

15. An attempt to reconcile the events of April 1980 with the earlier "Arc of Crisis" thesis can be found in Amos Perlmutter, "The Yemen Strategy," *The New Republic,* July 5 and 12, 1980. Perlmutter's story is, however, wide of the mark: it leaves out of account the fact that the Soviet Ambassador in Aden tried for three days prior to Abdul Fatah Ismail's ouster to convince Politburo's members he should stay, and it omits the central part played in Abdul Fatah's downfall by the failure of the Russians to provide adequate economic assistance to South Yemen. It is another case of the covert deductivism of so much writing on this area—pretending to discern some wider and ever-advancing Soviet "strategy" behind a pattern of events. Yet the events are themselves misread in order to "prove" the theory that had been assumed from the very beginning.

16. Overall accounts of the Ethiopian revolution are to be found in Rene Lefort, *Ethiopia, La Revolution Heretique* (Paris, 1981), and Marina and David Ottaway, *Ethiopia: Empire to Revolution* (New York: Holmes & Meier, 1978). See also Fred Halliday and Maxine Molyneux, *Revolution in Ethiopia* (London, 1981). For further, detailed and extremely well-informed, discussion of the origins of the military regime, see "The P.M.A.C.: Origins and Structure" by Pliny the Middle-Aged in *Ethiopianist Notes* 2, 3 (1978) (Part I) and *Northeast African Studies* 1, 1 (1979) (Part II).

17. Amnesty International, *Human Rights Violations in Ethiopia* (London: A.I., 1977).

18. For details of Soviet-Ethiopian divergences, see *Washington Post,* March 17, 1979; a reading of the Soviet press in the period between the outbreak of the revolution in February 1974 and the consolidation of the Moscow-Addis Abbaba alliance in 1977 shows the Russians giving voice to considerable doubts about the direction events were taking. Thus we find the veteran correspondent Valentin Korovikov writing in *Pravda* in May 1976, on the difficulties which the socialist transformation of Ethiopia will encounter: "This will be neither swift nor easy. About 90 percent of the population lives in the villages. The great majority of the people are illiterate. The country's per capita income is very low, and religious prejudices are still strong. All this demands a more careful and realistic appraisal of the situation by the authorities ... " *Pravda,* May 16, 1976, as translated in *Current Digest of the Soviet Press,* vol. 28, no. 20, p. 20.

19. On Soviet-Ethiopian divergences and Ethiopia's cautious opening to the West, see *The Guardian,* March 31, 1981.

Chapter VI

1. *Ethiopia and the Horn of Africa,* hearings before the Subcommittee

on African Affairs of Senate Foreign Relations Committee, Washington, 1976, p. 36.

2. The C.I.A.'s role in the 1953 coup in Iran has been documented in a variety of places; the most extensive, if not always most reliable, account is that of the main C.I.A. organizer of the operation, Kim Roosevelt, in *Counter-Coup* (New York, 1980).

3. The U.S. role in training SAVAK is discussed by former C.I.A. analyst Jesse Leaf in *International Herald Tribune*, January 8, 1979, and in Carl Kaplan and Fred Halliday, "The SAVAK-C.I.A. Connection," *The Nation*, March 1, 1980.

4. Kissinger's refusal to discuss the Somali offer is revealed by James Akins, former U.S. Ambassador to Saudi Arabia, in *Multinational Corporations and U.S. Foreign Policy*, U.S. Senate Subcommittee on Multinational Corporations, Part 14, Washington, 1976, pp. 43-434.

5. Author's interview with State Department Horn of Africa desk, May, 1979. On Cahill see *Newsweek*, September 26, 1977; and Jim Paul in *MERIP Reports* 62 (November, 1977), "Kevin Cahill: a Medical Macchiavelli," who describes the doctor as follows: "He is an experienced professional in the world of politics and diplomacy and has devoted his entire career to using medicine as an opening wedge for high level political action." I have analyzed U.S. policy in the Horn up to mid-1978 in "U.S. Policy in the Horn of Africa: *Aboulia* or Proxy Intervention?" *Review of African Political Economy* 10 (September-December, 1978).

6. On C.I.A. arms supplies to Somalia see *Seven Days*, March 19, 1978. Some of the strongest criticism of the U.S. mistakes in the Horn has come from Israel, which retains a permanent interest in supporting an anti-Arab Ethiopia. See Nimrod Novik, *On the Shores of Bab Al-Mandab: Soviet Diplomacy and Regional Dynamics* (Philadelphia: Foreign Policy Research Institute, 1979), p. 59.

7. Author's interview with Cuban Foreign Ministry officials, Havana, March, 1981.

8. *Proposed Aircraft Sales to Israel, Egypt, and Saudi Arabia,* hearings before the Committee on International Relations, House of Representatives, Washington, 1978, p. 35, 69. This evaluation was challenged by Rep. Paul Findley, a U.S. Congressman who has twice visited South Yemen, *ibid.,* p. 61.

9. For typical examples of such militaristic bit-chafing see Arnaud de Borchgrave, "Oman: In Dire Straits," *Newsweek,* September 24, 1979, and Captain Richard Stewart, U.S. Marine Corps, "Oman: The Next Crisis?" *Proceedings,* April, 1980, who writes: "If the United States draws a line against Soviet-controlled expansion in that area, as Sultan Qaboos urges and the United States seems willing to do now, it is possible that U.S. forces could be defending that line in the rugged frontier region of Southern Oman." This was wishful thinking.

10. The biggest group among the new specialists comprises mlitary and internal security experts. "They're crew-cut types who report to the embassy's defence section," an embassy source said. *International Herald Tribune,* December 15, 1978.

11. As of the end of 1980 it remained doubtful how successful that policy was being, especially given divergences over (a) Afghanistan; (b) the price 135

at which the Russians would buy Iranian gas and; (c) the role of the pro-Soviet Tudeh Party in Iran. See "Russian not getting far in courtship of Iran: Viewed by Many as 'Lesser Satan,' " *International Herald Tribune*, June 21-22, 1980.

12. Pakistani bases, used for military purposes by Afghan rebels, were reported at the following points along the border area: Chitral, Miramshah, Parachinar, Warsak, Spinwan, Zhob. It would appear that this form of Pakistani assistance *decreased* after the Soviet intervention, but that Egyptian and Western aid rose.

13. Chinese instructors were first detected in Pakistan assisting the Afghans when U.S. Drug Enforcement Agency personnel encountered people whom they at first thought were Hong Kong heroin smugglers; see Peter Niesewand in *McLean's* magazine (Toronto) April 30, 1979. U.S. military supplies to the rebels were first confirmed in February, 1980, and seem to have consisted of supplies of Russian equipment, of a kind matching that which the rebels were themselves capturing. Such supplies could have come from Egypt, which had previously been armed by the Russians, or from Israel, which captured a lot of Egyptian arms in 1967. As of mid-1980 the level of U.S. supplies did not appear to be very high. A much more concerted U.S. policy was the disinformation campaign waged from its embassies in Kabul and Delhi and upon which much of the world's press relied, so that levels of Soviet casualties were grossly exaggerated. For illuminating accounts of how U.S. officials rigged the news on Afghanistan see Philip Jacobsen in *The Sunday Times*, February 10, 1980, and July 27, 1980.

14. The remark of one senior British Foreign Office official is, in this context, quite revealing. Speaking of Western response to the Soviet intervention he said: "We discovered Afghanistan only after the Russians went in." The deputy chief of the mission at the U.S. Embassy in Kabul in the period 1951-53 later wrote: "During those two years, at least, the State Department showed absolutely no interest in Afghanistan or its possible pivotal role in East-West relations. I forwarded a number of reports to Washington raising some questions, but there was no response." (John E. Horner, *The Economist*, August 2, 1980.)

Chapter VII

1. Professor John Erickson, "Some Notes on the Soviet Score," Memorandum presented to the Foreign Affairs Committee, House of Commons, London, March 19, 1980. Erickson, the leading British authority on the Soviet military, identifies the rise of what he terms a "globalist approach" to foreign policy, marked by an "emphasis on *access* and *influence* rather than occupation and control" (pp. 35-36).

2. Independent information on the Soviet base facilities in Aden is not available but the main function seems to have been to act as a point through which Soviet crews (flown by Aeroflot to South Yemen) could replace personnel serving in the Indian Ocean and thereby avoid the need for the ships to make the long journey to home ports in the Black Sea or Far East. The majority of Soviet personnel are training South Yemenis in the use of new equipment, much of it, such as the SAM missile barrier around

Aden, a direct response to U.S. arms sales to Saudi Arabia. Reports of a new Soviet base on the island of Socotra, owned by South Yemen, have not been substantiated: indeed both U.S. State Department officials and British Foreign Office interviewed on this subject in early 1981 doubted the truth of these reports. "Anyone who thinks the Russians could have a base on Socotra has never looked at the *Red Sea Pilot*," remarked the British official, in an illusion to the monsoon storms, shoals and lack of natural harbor conditions around the island.

3. In the words of the Soviet dissident Roy Medvedev: "I have had conversations with several experts and observers who have told me that if the American Senate had been going to ratify SALT-II, if Western Europe had refused to take NATO cruise missiles as the U.S.S.R. requested and if the Soviet-Chinese talks had gone successfully, then the Soviet government would have found it very difficult to make the decision to go into Afghanistan," *New Left Review* 121 (May-June, 1980), p. 94.

4. Article 72 of the 1977 Soviet Constitution states: "Each Union Republic shall retain the right freely to secede from the U.S.S.R."

5. In both the Iraqi and Ethiopian cases, there remained divergences between the Russians and their local allies. In the former case, the Russians, who had previously given sympathy to the Kurds, were restrictive in their arms supply policy, and were later openly criticized by the Iraqis for this. In the case of Eritrea, the Russians continued to call for a "political solution" in Eritrea and held some discussions in Moscow with leaders of one guerrilla group, the Eritrean Liberation Front. While these Soviet reservations were resented by, respectively, Baghdad and Addis Abbaba, the balance of Soviet policy, and of Soviet material support, was definitely in favor of these governments.

6. Karen Dawisha, *op. cit.,* p. 13.

7. It would appear that a civilian faction of the Pakistani government, represented by Foreign Minister Agha Shahi, has favored negotiating with Kabul, but that the military, eager for increased support from Washington, have opposed this. The obvious inducement which the Afghan government could offer is recognition of the 1893 frontier between the two states, which Kabul has till now rejected.

8. *Sunday Times,* March 2, 1980. For useful background see Shahram Chubin, *Soviet Policy Towards Iran and the Gulf* (London: International Institute for Strategic Studies, 1980). Chubin's overall framework is a conventional enough one, with periodic references to Soviet "bullying": but the evidence he adduces points to different conclusions. He stresses both the caution of Soviet policy and the primacy of local political forces.

Conclusion

1. "The principle of peaceful coexistence between states with different social systems, as is well known, as nothing in common with class peace between the exploiters and the exploited, the colonialists and the victims of colonial oppression, or between the oppressors and the oppressed," Mikhail Suslov, Soviet Communist Party theoretician in *Kommunist,* July 21, 1975, as quoted in Stephen Kaplan, *Diplomacy of Power* (Washington, D.C.: Brookings Institution, 1981), p. 195.

APPENDIX I:
The Soviet View of the "Code of Conduct"*

Speaking in the Kremlin on April 27, Leonid Brezhnev, General Secretary of the Central Committee of the Communist Party of the Soviet Union and President of the Presidium of the U.S.S.R. Supreme Soviet, outlined a "code of conduct" in relation to young states, which, he said, the U.S.S.R. was always prepared to observe and which it recommended to the U.S.A. and other states.

"The present American administration, which is apt to see in all the events taking place in the world the 'hand of Moscow,' repeatedly launches appeals to the U.S.S.R. and its allies to agree on the observance of some 'code of rules or conduct' in relations with the young states of Africa, Asia and Latin America," said Leonid Brezhnev. "It is alleged that the world will be a calmer place in that eventuality.

"What can one say to this?

"If what is meant is certain 'rules' which would perpetuate imperialist brigandage, *diktat* with regard to the states mentioned, the establishment of certain 'spheres of influence,' etc., then, of course, we shall never agree to that. It runs counter to the principles of our policy.

"At the same time the U.S.S.R. has always been and is in favor of strict and complete observance of the principle of equality and the generally recognized standards of international law in relations among all states, such standards as, for instance, those that are embodied in the United Nations Charter, in the Helsinki Final Act or, say, in the well-known agreements of the 1970s between the U.S.S.R. and the U.S.A., agreements which are, deplorably, now being flouted by the U.S. authorities.

"We believe that the application of these standards to relations with the young states of the three continents, in

*Source: *Soviet News,* April 28, 1981, published by the Soviet Embassy in London.

the present situation, means roughly the following:

Recognition of the right of each people to decide its domestic affairs without outside interference; renunciation of attempts to establish any forms of domination or hegemony over them or to include them in the 'sphere of interest' of any power.

Strict respect for the territorial integrity of those countries: inviolability of their frontiers. No outside support for any separatist movements aimed at partitioning those countries.

Unconditional recognition of the right of each African, Asian and Latin American state to play an equal part in international life and to develop relations with any countries.

Complete and unconditional recognition of the sovereignty of those states over their natural resources and also *de facto* recognition of their complete equality in international economic relations, support for their efforts aimed at eliminating the vestiges of colonialism and at eradicating racism and apartheid in accordance with the well-known decisions of the United Nations.

Respect for the status of non-alignment chosen by the majority of African, Asian and Latin American states. Renunciation of attempts to draw them into the military-political blocs of big powers.

"Such is the 'code of conduct' that we recognize and are always prepared to observe. And we recommend this to the United States, other permanent members of the United Nations Security Council and, naturally, other states. Then the world will really become more tranquil and the peoples will be able to be more confident about the future," Leonid Brezhnev continued.

APPENDIX II:
The Persian Gulf:
Soviet Proposals*

Excerpts from speech by Leonid Brezhnev before the Indian Parliament on December 10, 1980.

The situation in Asia now is, unfortunately, disquieting.

The situation in the Middle East, where attempts are being made to impose upon Arab countries capitulatory deals and to make them resign themselves to the flouting of their fundamental national interests, is still explosive.

Tension persists in South-East Asia, where the forces of imperialism and their accomplices are conducting a policy of setting South-East Asian states against each other and are preventing in every way the establishment of relations of good-neighborliness between them.

The Iraqi-Iranian conflict, tragic in its senselessness, is continuing. This is a patent example of how dangerous it is for countries which are not yet strong enough to find themselves in millstones of imperialist policy.

Who gains from this war? Certainly neither Iraq nor Iran. They will get only a ravaged economy and large losses of manpower. Yet it is already clear that somebody has gained from the war. Foreign military penetration of the Middle and Near East is intensively under way, in full view of the whole world. The unity of the Arab world is being shaken, to the joy of the enemies of the Arab peoples. There are also calculations to weaken the anti-imperialist direction of the policy of both Iran and Iraq. And for all that, the two neighboring peoples are paying with their blood.

This is why the U.S.S.R. resolutely stands for a peaceful settlement of the conflict. We denounce any attempts to have it protracted, to pour oil on the flames of war one way or another. As we understand, India's position is similar to ours.

The opponents of the normalization of the international climate and initiators of the arms race now not infrequently refer in justification of their actions to the situation in Afghanistan. But by doing so, if one thinks this over, they are taking a very peculiar stand.

They raise a world-wide hullabaloo about a "Soviet threat," either to Pakistan or to Persian Gulf countries, or God knows whom, although they are well aware that no such threat exists whatsoever.

They stridently demand the cessation of Soviet military aid to Afghanistan, while, in fact, doing everything to hinder this. They are seeking to preserve tension and prevent the normalization of the situation. They continue to send armed gangs into Afghanistan and fear like death an understanding between Afghanistan and it, neighbors, especially Pakistan.

In a word, the stand of these gentlemen is, to put it mildly, insincere.

Deception, however, will not get one very far. Life in Afghanistan is gradually becoming and will continue to become increasingly more normal and peaceful, and the fog of misinformation will gradually disperse. And then, one can assume, Afghanistan's southern neighbors will realize that a good neighborly accord with the Afghan government is the only real path. As a result, conditions will emerge for a complete political normalization of the situation, including the withdrawal of Soviet troops from Afghanistan.

Let me assure you, esteemed Members of Parliament, that the Soviet Union is precisely for such a development of events (and we fully support the reasonable proposals on this score made by the government of Afghanistan).

The region of the Persian Gulf and the Indian Ocean is becoming an increasingly more dangerous center of international tension. On the invented pretext of the protection of their "vital interests," powers situated many thousands of kilometers away from the region have concentrated a military armada there and are intensively building up armaments, expanding the network of their military bases, and subjecting to pressure and threats the small countries which do not follow in their wake.

Attempts are being made to justify such actions by talk of the "Soviet threat" to this region's oil wealth. It goes without saying that this is a sheer fabrication, and its authors are well aware of that. The U.S.S.R. does not intend to encroach either on Middle East oil or its supply route.

It is certainly not all the same to us what is taking place in an area so close to our frontiers. We want a normal, calm situation to be created there. We advocate the doctrine of peace and security, which offsets the imperialist doctrine of aggression and *diktat* against the Persian Gulf countries.

These are not mere words. This is our real policy. We propose to the United States, other Western powers, China, Japan and all states which show interest in this, to agree on the following mutual obligations:

- not to establish foreign military bases in the area of the Persian Gulf and adjacent islands, and not to deploy nuclear or any other weapons of mass destruction there;
- not to use and not to threaten the use of force against the countries of the Persian Gulf area, and not to interfere in their internal affairs;
- to respect the non-aligned status chosen by Persian Gulf states, and not to draw them into military groupings with the participation of nuclear powers;
- to respect the sovereign right of the states of the region to their natural resources;
- not to raise any obstacles or threats to normal trade exchange and the use of sea lanes linking the states of the region with other countries of the world.

We believe that such an accord, with the states of the region themselves, naturally, because full-fledged parties to it, would meet their vital interests. It would be a reliable guarantee ensuring their sovereign rights and security.

Let me express the hope that this proposal will meet with understanding and support on the part of peace-loving India.

The Soviet Union is a staunch champion of the idea that the Indian Ocean can be turned into a zone of peace.

We are ready to work actively together with other interested states in this direction. We believe that the Indian Ocean has been and remains the sphere of vital interests of the states located on its shores, but not of any other states.

We are also ready to welcome any other initiatives which would lead to the relaxation of tension, which would be prompted by concern for the strengthening of peace in Asia or any other continent.

IPS PUBLICATIONS

Research Guide to Current
Military and Strategic Affairs
By William M. Arkin

The first comprehensive guide to public information sources on the U.S. military establishment. Soviet and other foreign military affairs, and global strategic issues. Provides descriptions of all basic research tools. Topics include: the U.S. military defense policy and posture; the defense budget; arms sales and military aid; weapons systems; NATO arms control and disarmament; and intelligence operations. Indispensable for anyone interested in current military and strategic affairs. $15.95 (paper, $7.95).

Real Security: Restoring American
Power in a Dangerous Decade
By Richard J. Barnet

"*Real Security* is a *tour de force,* a gift to the country. One of the most impassioned and effective arguments for sanity and survival that I have ever read."—Dr. Robert L. Heilbroner

"An inspired and inspiring achievement . . . a first salvo in the campaign to turn our current security policies—diplomatic, military, and economic—in the direction of rationality. It may well be the basic statement around which opponents of unalloyed confrontation can gather. It will have great impact."—John Marshall Lee, Vice Admiral, USN (Ret.)

"As a summary of the critical literature on the arms race, Barnet's brief essay is an important antidote to hawkish despair."—*Kirkus Reviews*

$10.95 (paper, $4.95).

The Counterforce Syndrome: A Guide
to U.S. Nuclear Weapons and Strategic Doctrine
By Robert C. Aldridge

This study discloses the shift from "deterrence" to "counterforce" in U.S. strategic doctrine. A thorough, newly-revised summary and analysis of U.S. strategic nuclear weapons and military policy including descriptions of MIRVs, MARVs, Trident systems, cruise missiles, and M-X missiles in relation to the aims of a U.S. first-strike attack. $4.95.

Dubious Specter:
A Skeptical Look at the Soviet Nuclear Threat
By Fred Kaplan

Do the Soviets really threaten American ICBMs with a devastating surprise attack? Will Soviet military doctrine lead the Russians to threaten nuclear war in order to wring concessions from the West? Do Soviet leaders think they can fight and win a nuclear war? Fred Kaplan separates the myths from the realities about U.S. and Soviet nuclear stockpiles and strategies and provides the necessary background for understanding current debates on arms limitations and military costs. $4.95.

The New Generation of Nuclear Weapons
By Stephen Daggett

An updated summary of strategic weapons, including American and Soviet nuclear hardware. These precarious new technologies may provoke startling shifts in strategic policy, leading planners to consider fighting "limited nuclear wars" or developing a preemptive first strike capability. $3.00.

The Rise and Fall of the 'Soviet Threat':
Domestic Sources of the Cold War Consensus
By Alan Wolfe

A timely essay demonstrating that American fear of the Soviet Union tends to fluctuate according to domestic factors as well as in relation to the military and foreign policies of the USSR. Wolfe contends that recurring features of American domestic politics periodically coalesce to spur anti-Soviet sentiment, contributing to increased tensions and dangerous confrontations.

"At this moment, one could hardly want a more relevant book."— *Kirkus Reviews*. $4.95.

The Giants
Russia and America
By Richard Barnet

An authoritative, comprehensive account of the latest stage of the complex U.S.-Soviet relationship; how it came about, what has changed, and where it is headed.

"A thoughtful and balanced account of American-Soviet relations. Barnet goes beyond current controversies to discuss the underlying challenges of a relationship that is crucial to world order."— Cyril E. Black, Director, Center for International Studies, Princeton University. $4.95.

Toward World Security:
A Program for Disarmament
By Earl C. Ravenal

This proposal argues that new strategic weapons systems and increasing regional conflicts should prompt the U.S. to take independent steps toward disarmament including nondeployment of counterforce weapons. $2.00.

Supplying Repression: U.S. Support
for Authoritarian Regimes Abroad
By Michael T. Klare and Cynthia Arnson

A comprehensive discussion of the programs and policies through which the U.S. supports police and internal security forces in repressive Third World countries.

"Very important, fully documented indictment of U.S. role in supplying rightist Third World governments with the weaponry and know-how of repression."—*The Nation.* $9.95 (paper, $4.95).

Beyond the Vietnam Syndrome:
U.S. Interventionism in the 1980s
By Michael T. Klare

A study of the emergence of a new U.S. interventionist military policy. Shows how policymakers united to combat the "Vietnam Syndrome"—the public's resistance to American military involvement in future Third World conflicts—and to relegitimate the use of military force as an instrument of foreign policy. Includes a close look at the Pentagon's "Rapid Deployment Force," and a study of comparative U.S. Soviet transcontinental intervention capabilities. $4.95.

Resurgent Militarism
By Michael T. Klare and the Bay Area Chapter
of the Inter-University Committee

An analysis of the origins and consequences of the growing militaristic fervor which is spreading from Washington across the nation. The study examines America's changing strategic position since Vietnam and the political and economic forces which underlie the new upsurge in militarism. $2.00.

After the Shah
By Fred Halliday

Important background information on the National Front, the Tudeh Party, the religious opposition and many other groups whose policies and programs will determine Iran's future. $2.00.

The Lean Years
Politics in the Age of Scarcity
By Richard J. Barnet

A lucid and startling analysis of basic global resources: energy, non-fuel minerals, food, water, and human labor. The depletion and maldistribution of supplies bodes a new global economic, political and military order in the 1980s.

"... brilliantly informed book ... cogent, aphoristic pulling together of the skeins of catastrophic scarcity in 'the coming postpetroleum world ... "—*Publishers Weekly*. $12.95.

Feeding the Few:
Corporate Control of Food
By Susan George

The author of *How the Other Half Dies* has extended her critique of the world food system which is geared towards profit not people. This study draws the links between the hungry at home and those abroad exposing the economic and political forces pushing us towards a unified global food system. $4.95.

Global Reach:
The Power of the Multinational Corporations
By Richard Barnet and Ronald Müller

"A searching, provocative inquiry into global corporations . . . Barnet and Muller are trenchant and telling in their discussion of the possible end of the nation-state, and have some penetrating views on 'economic imperialism' and future changes in employment patterns and the standard of living under the domination of the global oligopolists."—*Publishers Weekly*. $7.95.

South Africa:
Foreign Investment and Apartheid
By Lawrence Litvak, Robert DeGrasse,
and Kathleen McTigue

A critical examination of the argument that multinationals and foreign investment operate as a force for progressive change in South Africa. "Its concise and well-documented debunking of the myth that foreign investment will eventually change the system of exploitation and repression in South Africa deserves wide readership .. Highly recommended."—*Library Journal*. $3.95.

The Crisis of the Corporation
By Richard Barnet

Now a classic, this essay analyzes the power of the multinational corporations which dominate the U.S. economy, showing how the growth of multinationals inevitably results in an extreme concentration of economic and political power in a few hands. The result, according to Barnet, is a crisis for democracy itself. $1.50.

Decoding Corporate Camouflage:
U.S. Business Support for Apartheid
By Elizabeth Schmidt
Foreword by Congressman Ronald Dellums

By exposing the decisive role of U.S. corporations in sustaining apartheid, this study places highly-touted employment "reforms" in the context of the systematic economic exploitation and political repression of the black South African majority.

' .. forcefully presented."—*Kirkus Reviews.* $4.95.

A Continent Beseiged:
Foreign Military Activities in Africa Since 1975
By Daniel Volman

A study of the growing military involvement of the two superpowers and their allies in Africa. $2.00.

The Nicaraguan Revolution:
A Personal Report
By Richard R. Fagen

Tracing the history of the Nicaraguan Revolution, Fagen focuses on six legacies that define current Nicaraguan reality: armed struggle; internationalization of the conflict; national unity; democratic visions; death, destruction and debts; and political bankruptcy. This primer on the state of Nicaraguan politics and economics provides an insightful view of the Sandinist quest for power and hegemony. The report contains twenty photographs by Marcelo Montecino and appendices with the basic documents necessary for understanding contemporary Nicaraguan affairs. $4.00.

Chile: Economic 'Freedom'
and Political Repression
By Orlando Letelier

A trenchant analysis by the former leading official of the Allende government who was assassinated by the Pinochet junta. This essay demonstrates the necessary relationship between an economic development model which benefits only the wealthy few and the political terror which has reigned in Chile since the overthrow of the Allende regime. $1.00.

Assassination on Embassy Row
By John Dinges and Saul Landau

A devastating political document that probes all aspects of the Letelier-Moffitt assassinations, interweaving the investigations of the murder by the FBI and the Institute.

"... An engrossing study of international politics and subversion... ."—*Kirkus Reviews*. $14.95.

Human Rights and Vital Needs
By Peter Weiss

Delivered one year after the assassination of Orlando Letelier and Ronni Karpen Moffitt, this extraordinary address commemorates them by calling for a human rights policy that includes not only political and civil rights, but economic, social, and cultural rights as well. $1.00.

The Federal Budget
and Social Reconstruction
Marcus Raskin, Editor

This study describes the Federal Budget, sets new priorities for government spending and presents alternative policies for defense, energy, health and taxation.

"The issuance of this report is a major political event and a challenge to mainstream ideology. It should be widely purchased." —*Library Journal*. $8.95.

Postage and Handling:
All orders must be prepaid. For delivery within the USA, please add 15% of order total. For delivery outside the USA, add 20%. Standard discounts available upon request.

Please write the Institute for Policy Studies, 1901 Que Street, N.W., Washington, D.C. 20009 for our complete catalog of publications and films.

DATE DUE